CO-DESIGNING PUBLICS

The book is dedicated to Elahe,
for her extraordinary love.

Acknowledgements:

I would like to thank Juan Usubillaga, the Network Administrator of the Co-Designing Publics international research network, for his uncompromising dedication, infectious passion, and tireless efforts. I am also deeply grateful to my fellow members of the network, who are all authors in this book and who contributed immensely to the creation and carrying through of this research project from its inception. At Cardiff University, Samantha Johnson has been an incredible pillar of understanding and unwavering support throughout the process. Finally, at ORO Editions, Jake Anderson has been an excellent colleague and true friend of the book.
Thank you all.

TABLE OF CONTENTS

CO-DESIGNING PUBLICS:

A THEORETICAL AND INVESTIGATIVE OVERVIEW

ASEEM INAM

I am Professor and Chair in Urban Design at Cardiff University in the UK, and Director of TRULAB: Laboratory for Designing Urban Transformation, which was founded in New York City. I describe myself as an activist-scholar-practitioner, because being an activist means coming from a mindset that recognizes real change must be systemic and long term, because being a scholar means acknowledging the significance of deep understanding (i.e., research) and of principle- and pattern-making (i.e., theory), because being a practitioner means believing in direct action and intervention in cities, and because it is the intertwining of these three aspects that leads to urban transformation. I am also the Principal Investigator of our "Co-Designing Publics" international research network, funded by a grant awarded to us by the UK Arts and Humanities Research Council. The following series of essays in this book are public conversations, based on edited and updated excerpts from the international symposium that was in conducted online in September 2021 with over 350 registered participants.

PREMISES

The 21st century is truly the urban century by any measure. There exist different ways of understanding and measuring what is the "urban,"[1] but what they all share in common is the growing and increasingly critical significance of the role of cities in our world. Given the multiple crises that cities face, such as the climate emergency, urban inequality, inadequate infrastructure, and the COVID-19 global pandemic, this presentation focuses on developing innovative ways in which processes of co-designing publics and producing the public realm on an ongoing basis can more effectively help address these crises.

Three notes of clarification before I continue.

First, I deploy the term "urbanism" rather than "urban design" for a number of reasons. Conventional urban design has a long history of having an overly narrow and constrained definition as essentially architecture at a larger scale, with its attendant obsessions with aesthetics and three-dimensional objects while overlooking the larger political-economic structures and dynamics that actually shape cities. Urbanism from a design perspective connotes not only a significant shift in terminology but one in attitude towards a far more critical, transdisciplinary, and engaged approach to the design of cities. Furthermore, a potent question to ask ourselves is not so much "What is urban design?" but "What can urbanism be?" because the second question leads to answers that are future oriented, plural, and based on a much wider range of critical and creative possibilities.

Second, I utilize what I call "categories of convenience." These categories enable us to specify particular types of phenomena, to investigate them in their contexts, and to better understand their relationalities, all the while acknowledging that such categories contain overlaps and fuzzy boundaries. Examples of such categories of convenience that are relevant here are:

- global south versus the global north.
- the public realm versus the private realm; and
- spatial versus non-spatial aspects of cities.

Third, I will share some images in this presentation that are suggestive about

Figure 1.1
Dhobi Ghat, Mahalakshmi, Mumbai.
Source: Aseem Inam, 2013.

possible implications for urban practices from this theoretical discussion, rather than making a one-to-one literal shift from theory to practice. The images are there as visual backgrounds in order to invoke the power of theory to reflect, to understand, and to suggest pathways towards transformative practice.

PUBLIC REALM

Cities are amongst humanity's greatest creations, and the public realm is arguably their most significant aspect. The public realm is what makes a city so rich, so complex, and so full of potential. The starting point for examining the public realm is the fact that the city should belong to everyone, regardless of race, class, or gender. In reality, uneven access to resources and to power means that some individuals and groups are more privileged and influential

than others, especially in terms of exercising their rights or actively participating in democracy.[2] At the same time, as much as the current public realm largely reflects and embodies such imbalances of power, it is also the potent site of resistances, contestations, and alternatives to the mainstream status quo. Such alternatives help to illuminate the full potential of the public realm and of a city that can be truly democratic, in every sense of the term.

There is an argument to be made about a differing private realm versus a public realm. One way of thinking about the private realm is that it is largely the realm of the individual and that the essence of the private is the absence of others.[3] On the other hand, the public realm is largely the realm of the encounter with the other and of the collective. Spatially, being inside one's home is not the same experience as being on the street. Even online, one tends to have more of a public persona on social media such as Twitter and Facebook. While they are different, the private and public realms do intersect and interact.

What makes the public realm particularly potent is that it is the realm of the "other," par excellence. The public realm consists of spatial networks constituted by places of encounter and interactions of bodies, cultures, and ideas. Thus, the most significant aspect of the public realm is the fact that it is public. There are two aspects of defining the many meanings of the public that are most relevant here. One is that it is "of or relating to the people as a whole; that belongs to, affects, or concerns the community or the nation," and the other is that it is "open to general observation, view, or knowledge; existing, performed, or carried out without concealment, so that all may see or hear."[4] From this perspective, the public realm is arguably the most significant aspect of the city because it speaks to the notion of the city as sets of overlapping and intersecting communities.

Figure 1.2
Union Square, Manhattan, New York City. Source: Aseem Inam, 2015.

The vast potential of the public realm lies in its capacity to act as a catalyst for interactively and collaboratively generating hope by deepening understanding, for building solidarity, for creating dreams, and for pursuing transformative actions. While the public realm is spatially grounded at multiple scales in specific geographic contexts, it is also constantly evolving because the urbanism of a city is constantly in flux.[5] My own investigation into the public realm begins with its spatial manifestations, but by no means do I end it there because the public realm reaches structurally into the dynamics of the spatial political-economy of the city and reaches temporally into its production and reproduction over time. Direct engagement with these aspects is what I mean by the spatial production of the public realm. Thus, space as a starting point matters a great deal. For example, public life in streets and other public spaces is an inexorable part of a vibrant city culture. In addition, rather than being overdetermined in their specifications, the buildings, open spaces, and infrastructures of urbanism should allow for flexibility and change.

Public spaces such as squares, streets, and parks tend to be defined and bounded spatially and administratively. The public realm speaks more to interconnected spatial networks that contain such public spaces and the flows that they enable. The best example of this is the sidewalk (also known as the footpath or pavement), which truly embodies the everyday public realm because in most cities it is the most frequented public space by the largest variety of people. Even the most privileged have to make the journey from their limousine to the front door of their luxury apartment building when their chauffeur drops them off, thereby traversing the sidewalk in the process. The public realm also integrates less obvious and more informal public spaces such as farmer's markets and skateboard parks into a city's network of publicness.

I challenge the standard notion of public space as more or less simply a container for human activity, a notion that continues to pervade conventional design thinking. In fact, the exclusion of some groups from democratic processes via their failures to attain recognition in public space underlines the critical importance of materiality.[6] Although many scholars recognize the democratic character of public space, this idea is also contested, as public space has paradoxically long been a site of exploitation, oppression, and prohibition for women, ethnic minorities, gays and lesbians, the elderly and young, the homeless, and people with disabilities. At the same time, public space remains the most important site where public claims can be made visible and contested. In order to fully understand this critical aspect of public space as part of a larger public realm, we have to view it as part of its spatial political-economy.

Spatial political-economy signifies two key aspects directly related to urbanism. One is the set of power structures and dynamics that exert influence on how, why, by whom, and for whose benefit the city is produced and reproduced over time. Second, within this set of power structures and dynamics, are the decision-making processes and outcomes that result in urban priorities and human, financial, and material resource allocations towards urban interventions. Moreover, the concept of the spatial political-economy acknowledges that the production and reproduction of space do not simply represent aesthetic, technical, or policy interventions of conventional design practices; rather that they are profoundly ideological and political acts.[7] Some of the vast untapped potential of design in the context of urbanism can be unleashed by more fully embracing and engaging with the realities of this spatial political-economy.

Ultimately, one of the most significant design issues for cities is the design of its governance,[8] which extends equally to the public realm. Who designs the public realm over time, and by access to which types of resources? Who controls its spaces?

What is allowed? What is not allowed? Who benefits from it, and why or why not? Here, the question of power, examined through political-economic dynamics, is central to our understanding of the public realm.[9] Power is not only embedded deeply and expressed spatially,[10] but it is exercised on an ongoing basis through control. An especially significant way to examine the uneven distribution and wielding of power has been through the perspective of social justice.[11]

INFORMAL URBANISMS

A key aspect of my interest in the public realm is an understanding of the role of informal urbanisms. I use the term "informal urbanisms" broadly to describe a wide range of informal strategies and outcomes in the spatial production of the city. Informal urbanisms are not marginalized forms of places and practices; rather, they are central to understanding the logic of urbanism because they constitute debates about what is legal and illegal in the city, what is legitimate and illegitimate, and with what effects.[12] In fact, the informal and the formal are intertwined, with some clear delineations of coded regulations and mechanisms of finance (e.g., municipal budgets and bank loans), legality (e.g., planning regulations and public policies), and administration (e.g., institutionalized routines and procedures).[13]

Informal urbanisms are both procedural strategies and tangible outcomes that are deeply intertwined and should be understood as such, rather than as separate and discrete phenomena. In design terms, spatial products such as buildings, open spaces, and infrastructures emerge out of particular processes while further reinforcing those processes. In this context, what I mean by design is a direct and regular engagement and interaction with the material city–variously referred to as the built environment, urban landscape, or urban fabric–including and especially with its spatial political-economy, without which design would not be possible. For example, developer-led and profit-driven urbanism, in which land and property are primarily commodities to be bought, sold, and invested in, reflects the capitalist system that so dominates the economy and the political structure that enables it both locally and globally.

I propose an investigative approach towards informal urbanisms about what we do know, how we know, and what we don't know. Cities are highly complex and constantly changing, so even if we know a lot, we need to know more by digging deeper and stretching our understanding of informality. In recent decades, three schools of thought have emerged, with informal urbanisms being positioned within a dualist (i.e., marginal economic activities for low-income households distinct from modern capitalism), legalist (i.e., excluded from the modern economy due to adverse bureaucracy), and structuralist frameworks (i.e., subordinated economic units adversely related to formal enterprises within a capitalist economy).[14] In addition, informal practices extend beyond the urban poor to encompass the actions of different sectors including middle- and high-income urban residents, the state, and business interests.[15]

One of the significant repercussions of such a theoretical and methodological approach towards informal urbanisms is to recognize that citizens are agents of urbanization, not simply consumers of spaces developed and regulated by others.[16] They build their houses, neighborhoods, and urban districts step by step according to the resources they are able to put together at each moment in the process. Each phase involves a great amount of improvisation and bricolage, complex strategies and calculations, and constant imaginations of what a "home," a "neighborhood," and a "public realm" might look like.[17] I put these terms in quotation marks to signify that the meaning of home, neighborhood, and public realm may very well be something radically different from these concepts either theorized in the

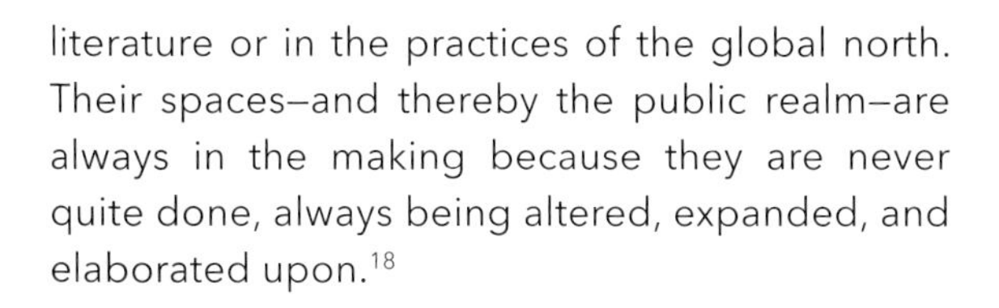

literature or in the practices of the global north. Their spaces–and thereby the public realm–are always in the making because they are never quite done, always being altered, expanded, and elaborated upon.[18]

CO-DESIGNING PUBLICS

The most potent aspect of the public realm lies in its capacity to co-design publics. Publics never simply exist; they are always created.[19] Publics are created (or co-designed by citizens themselves) out of groups of people who are made and remade by the actions of other people. For example, when there is a common concern or desire (that emerges out a crisis such as urban inequality, lack of affordable housing, inadequate infrastructure, or the COVID-19 global pandemic), there is a call to action and groups of people are willing to act upon those concerns or desires, and a public is created. A public is summoned into being. In this manner, co-designing publics is part of an ongoing process of designing and redesigning democracy with the city as its site and its context.[20] My work builds on this phenomenon to better understand how informal urbanisms in the public realm can become catalysts for co-designing publics.

As much as the design focus in urbanism tends to be on the creation of spatial products such as buildings, open spaces, and infrastructures,

Figure 1.3
Mural in the Ocupação São João in São Paulo. Source: Aseem Inam, 2016.

equally–or perhaps even more–formidable is design as a process of creative brainstorming and crafting radical imaginaries in the context of issue-based publics. Issues are rarely given, and if they are given, tend to be so in the broadest of terms, still requiring further inquiry to make them apparent and known. Discovery occurs through the process of inquiry, which can be characterized by directed research, analysis, reflection, and synthesis, which produces a whole that is able to be made apparent and known. Design also aids discovery through engagement with everyday materiality of the city as a datum as well as the ways in which the action-oriented sensibilities of design reveal much through critical reflection on the issue, the site of action, and its larger context. Even before that, critical design issues and problems are to be discovered rather than be given by a client.

The nuts and bolts of co-designing publics are far from smooth. Processes of co-designing publics draw citizens into vital urban realms (including spaces) where they encounter each other and engage in collective and meaningful negotiations about what kind of city they desire. These encounters build a shared sense of common purpose and solidarity among citizens. But the encounters also make citizens aware of the substantive differences among them, and they are forced to confront and manage these differences together. There are various ways of dealing with such differences. Anarchists are much more willing to see things work themselves out in the process of unfolding through our collective efforts, subject to ongoing revision and revitalization, rather than following a set course towards some imagined end goal.[21] Pragmatists advocate open-ended collaboration where what matters the most is ongoing conversations in which participants figure things out as they go along, a process that can yield new ways of thinking and new ways of doing.[22] Such a radically democratic approach can be excruciating but ultimately liberating, and shares similarities with the iterative and reflective processes of design.

Such an intensive and collaborative open-endedness is one of the ultimate promises of co-designing publics through informal urbanisms in the public realm. Informal urbanisms generate new modes of politics through practices that produce new kinds of citizens, claims, and contestations.[23] These politics tend to be rooted in the spatial production of the public realm, especially in collective residential spaces and their attendant neighborhood spaces. In many cities, social movements and grassroots organisations have created new discourses of rights and put forward demands that are at the basis of the rise of new citizenships, the formulation of new constitutions, the experimentation with new forms of local administration, and the invention of new approaches to social policy, planning, law, and citizen participation. Thus, informal urbanisms are both processes and products, which stems from my very definition of urbanism in the first place, as city-design-and-building processes and their spatial outcomes or products.[24] In fact, it privileges process over product not only because form and space emerge out of specific types of processes in particular contexts to the benefit of some more than others and because the city is always in process as buildings, spaces, and infrastructures age and are demolished, newly built, repaired, modified, and so forth in a series of never-ending activities.

The ultimate goal of co-designing publics via the public realm is radical democracy. Radical democracy is the process of exertion, where a path towards social justice might be opened in place of utopia, as a permanent means without end. Through this process, radical democracy is about emancipation, which can be understood as an awakening, a (re)discovery of power that is deeply rooted in processes of mobilization and transformation,[25] and since the city belongs to everyone, then we are all in this process of emancipation together.

GLOBAL SOUTH

I contextualize this discussion by paying particular attention to the cities of the global south, because place matters in shaping urban thinking and urban practice. There is an increasing interest in thinking and practicing *from* cities of the global south rather than just *about* them. Looking from the cities of the global south provokes specific types of inquiry because of the particular nature of their urbanism.[26]

The cities of the global south are mostly located geographically in the southern hemisphere in Africa, Asia, and Latin America. The cities of the global south also tend to be historically the oldest occupied cities as well as currently the fastest growing cities in the world. These cities are also where one finds empirical conditions of precarity, in which large majorities of the population are politically, economically, and ecologically vulnerable.[27]

Looking from cities of the global south, then, points to certain characteristics of urban practice in those contexts, such as fluidity, uncertainty, and speculative action. These prevalent characteristics challenge all the certainties that evidence-based urban policy takes for granted: that systems will work as they should, that people will act predictably, and that the rules of the game are fair and stable.

In this manner, the view from the global south challenges dominant forms of

Figure 1.4
Muro da Gentileza,
Rio de Janeiro.
Source: Elahe
Karimnia, 2016.

knowledge and practice. This view is especially timely because both the COVID-19 global pandemic and its policy responses reveal the precarity of its cities by exacerbating the class inequalities and structural racisms upon which many of them have been built, including through deeply rooted legacies of colonialism. However, the cities of the global south are also filled with the types of plural and overlapping collectivities and density of interchanges that are at the heart of co-designing publics.[28]

LOOKING BACK . . . AND LOOKING AHEAD

In the Co-Designing Publics research network, we have been investigating and exploring these ideas by talking to, listening, and learning from each other. We were fortunate to have a number of distinguished and passionate scholar-practitioners from universities around the world:

- Dr. Aseem Inam, Cardiff University, UK;
- Dr. Charlotte Lemanski, University of Cambridge, UK;
- Dr. Melanie Lombard, University of Sheffield, UK;
- Dr. Neha Sami, Indian Institute of Human Settlements, India;
- Dr. AbdouMaliq Simone, University of Sheffield, UK;
- Dr. Simon Springer, University of Newcastle, Australia;
- Dr. Fernando Lara, University of Texas, USA; and
- Mr. Juan Usubillaga, Cardiff University, UK.

We are also fortunate to have a number of extremely dedicated and highly accomplished activist-practitioners from six different cities in the global south:

- Ms. Nalini Shekar and Mr. Akbar A., Hasiru Dala, Bengaluru;
- Ms. Elisa Sutanudjaja, Rujak Center for Urban Studies, Jakarta;
- Ms. Evaniza Rodrigues, União Nacional por Moradia Popular, Sao Paulo;
- Ms. Sopheap Chak, Cambodian Center for Human Rights, Phnom Penh;
- Ms. Lorna Fuller and Mr. Gabriel Klaasen, Project 90 by 2030, Cape Town, working with Dr. Jiska de Groot, University of Cape Town; and
- Mr. Alexander Lopez, Asociación Mejorando Vidas, Cali, working with Dr. Carlos Tobar, Universidad Javeriana Cali.

The primary objective of this research network is to bring together a unique mix of scholars, activists, and practitioners to discuss and debate discourses from scholarly research, case studies of grassroots activism, and design ideas for future action. The contextual grounding of these discourses in cities of the global south enables the network to focus on learning how socially innovative practices such as informal strategies and designing new publics operate around urban issues such as affordable housing and homelessness, violence and peace, sustainable and equitable energy systems, right to the city and cooperative models of property ownership, and the role of women in the informal economy. These stimulating conversations, which are a mix of workshops, podcasts, and final symposium, are the core activities for building this research network.

I now conclude with some final reflections on the ideas we have investigated thus far in this network. The real goal of producing and reproducing the public realm is to enable the ongoing co-design of publics, such that we move rapidly towards a far more just, equitable, and radically democratic city for all, especially for those who are marginalized. Co-design–with its direct engagement in the spatial and non-spatial aspects of urbanism and its inherent creative thinking and interdisciplinary approaches–is ideal for discovering and articulating radical imaginaries for the public realm. Scholars from different perspectives agree that hope lies in these ongoing processes and informal aspects of the public realm. Hope for designing the truly equitable future of our cities might thus very well reside in this messy; multi-faceted; and ultimately, political, nature of the spatial production and reproduction of cities, rather than in professionalized urbanisms.[29]

We can already see glimpses of a powerful new urban society in the midst of precarity. While they may seem fleeting and fragmented, they are still urban practices of social autogestion and spatial appropriation undertaken by real inhabitants. As we are already doing in our research network, we can closely examine these practices in their specific contexts, compare them across contexts, exchange experiences and ideas, and try to extrapolate to generate common understandings and new knowledge. We can use this new knowledge as a lens to help us see better and further because such practices can be difficult to acknowledge in the current spatial political-economies of corporatism and neoliberalism. Moreover, we can–together, as co-designed publics–use these understandings and tools to move toward a new horizon of radical democracy. Such examples abound. We have to learn–collaboratively–to see them; to understand them; to nurture them; and ultimately, we have to *be* them.

Question: At the very beginning of your presentation, you said something that I found quite powerful which is that, instead of focusing on what urban design is, we should talk about what urbanism can be, and this is because the conversation should be future-oriented. So, connecting that to what you were saying about informal urbanisms, can you talk a little bit more about the role of informal urbanisms in defining what the future of the city can be?

Aseem Inam: I think even though there's a lot of research and a lot of practices in informal urbanisms, there's still a lot of room to understand and to learn from them, because cities are large, complex, and always changing. There's still room for further understanding how citizens create cities for themselves on an ongoing basis and at what scales. Among the most remarkable creations are informal settlements, which are amazing creations by people who have very limited access to resources and who face incredible challenges, but that also embody the creative thinking that goes into creating such spaces. They can also be excellent examples of sustainability, where some of the smallest ecological footprints in the world are of people who live in informality. I would say the main point is how citizens get together with minimal resources and minimal access to power, and how they create spaces which, while rife with challenges, are also incredibly appropriate. Statistically, the vast majority of the world's population–which is about 85 percent or so–lives in the global south and in many of those cities, a large percentage of people live in informal settlements or informal conditions. So, even empirically, it's a massive phenomenon that we need to better understand, to work with, and of course, to transform in a sensitive manner. It's a big part of the design of future cities.

Question: To what extent can informal urbanisms be a catalyst for co-designing publics?

Aseem Inam: Your question gets to the heart of one of the main discussions we've been having. Informality expresses itself in many different ways as spaces, but also as strategies and processes, how people come together to figure things out. For example: one time I was working in Toronto, Canada, with a women's group. It was an immigrant women's group; they were not a legal organization and they didn't have proper funding, but they did amazing things in informal ways by coming together, working with the city, and trying things out. I think informal urbanisms can be just incredible ways of getting things done, and I think we need to understand that more because there's a lot of untapped potential there.

Question: With regard to the goals of this Co-Designing Publics research network, what is the target audience? Is it the professionals involved in design and spatial production so as to make their work more political and inclusive, or is it the various public groups, the "publics" as you describe them, so as to enable their empowerment?

Aseem Inam: Our target audience consists of all the ones you mentioned, and more.

ENDNOTES

1 For example, see:
United Nations:
www.un.org/development/desa/en/news/population/2018-revision-of-world-urbanization-prospects.html
European Commission:
www.reuters.com/article/us-global-cities/everything-weve-heard-about-global-urbanization-turns-out-to-be-wrong-researchers-idUSKBN1K21UU
NYU Marron Institute:
www.marroninstitute.nyu.edu/working-papers/our-not-so-urban-world
Urban Theory Lab:
www.urbantheorylab.net/site/assets/files/1016/2011_brenner_schmid.pdf

2 James Holston, *Insurgent Citizenship: Disjunctions of Democracy and Modernity in Brazil* [Princeton: Princeton University Press, 2008].

3 Hannah Arendt, *The Human Condition*, second edition [Chicago: University of Chicago Press, 1998].

4 Oxford English Dictionary,
www-oed-com.abc.cardiff.ac.uk, 2020.

5 Aseem Inam, *Designing Urban Transformation* [London and New York: Routledge, 2014].

6 Simon Springer, "Public Space as Emancipation: Meditations on Anarchism, Radical Democracy, Neoliberalism and Violence." *Antipode*, volume 43, number 2, pages 540–42, 2011.

7 Alexander Cuthbert, *Understanding Cities*: Method in Urban Design, London and New York: Routledge, 2011.

8 Gerald Frug, "The Architecture of Governance," paper [Austin: University of Texas, 2011].

9 Robert Dahl, *Who Governs? Democracy and Power in an American City*, 2nd edition [New Haven: Yale University Press, 2005].

10 Setha Low and Neil Smith, editors, *The Politics of Public Space* [New York and London: Routledge, 2006].

11 Don Mitchell, *The Right to the City: Social Justice and the Fight for Public Space* [New York and London: Guilford Press, 2003].

12 Aseem Inam, "Reclaiming Urban Practice for India: What Can Design Teach Us?," in *Future of Cities: Planning, Infrastructure, and Development*, edited by Ashok Kumar and D.S. Meshram [Routledge: London, 2022], pages 177-202.

13 Aseem Inam, "Designing New Practices of Transformative Urbanism: An Experiment in Toronto," *Urban Design International*, volume 24, pages 60–74, 2019.

14 Nicola Banks, Melanie Lombard, and Diana Mitlin, "Urban Informality as a Site of Critical Analysis," *The Journal of Critical Studies*, volume 56, issue 2: pages 223–38, 2019.

15 Ananya Roy, "Why India Cannot Plan Its Cities: Informality, Insurgence and the Idiom of Urbanization," *Planning Theory*, volume 8, number 1: pages 76-87, 2009.

16 Teresa Caldeira, "Peripheral urbanization: Autoconstruction, Transversal Logics, and Politics in Cities of the Global South," *Environment and Planning D: Society and Space*, volume 35, number 1: pages 3-20, 2017.

17 Jonathan Silver, "Incremental Infrastructures: Material Improvisation and Social Collaboration Across Post-Colonial Accra," *Urban Geography*, volume 35, number 6: pages 788-804, 2014.

18 Aseem Inam, "Beyond Objects: City as Flux," in *Designing Urban Transformation* [New York and London: Routledge, 2014], pages 60-111.

19 John Dewey, *The Public and Its Problems: An Essay in Political Inquiry*, edited and annotated by Melvin Rogers [Athens OH: Swallow Press, 2016].

20 Mark Purcell, "For John Dewey (and Very Much Also for Contemporary Critical Theory)," *Urban Geography*, volume 38, number 4: pages 495-501, 2017.

21 Simon Springer, "We Are the Inferno: A Conversation on the Anarchist Roots of Geography," interview by Alexander Reid Ross for *CrimethInc*, 2017, www.crimethinc.com/2017/08/10/anarchistgeography.

22 John Dryzek, "Pragmatism and Democracy: In Search of Deliberative Publics, *Journal of Speculative Philosophy*," volume 18, number 1: pages 72-79.

23 Teresa Caldeira, "Peripheral Urbanization: Autoconstruction, Transversal Logics, and Politics in Cities of the Global South," *Environment and Planning D: Society and Space*, volume 35, number 1: pages 3-20, 2017.

24 As I explain in Aseem Inam, *Designing Urban Transformation* [London and New York: Routledge, 2014], the hyphens suggest that conventional design practices (i.e., intentions that are embodied in drawings and models) and conventional building practices (i.e., implementations that are embodied in construction and modification) are in fact continuous processes, and that conventional spatial products (e.g., buildings, open spaces, infrastructures) are actually results of such processes.

25 Simon Springer, "Public Space as Emancipation: Meditations on Anarchism, Radical Democracy, Neoliberalism and Violence," *Antipode*, volume 43, number 2, pages 540-42, 2011.

26 Gautam Bhan, "Notes on a Southern Urban Practice," *Environment and Urbanization*, volume 31, issue 2: pages 639-54, 2019.

27 AbdouMaliq Simone and Edgar Pieterse, *New Urban Worlds: Inhabiting Dissonant Times* [New York: John Wiley and Sons, 2017].

28 Gautam Bhan, Teresa Caldeira, Kelly Gillespie, and AbouMaliq Simone, "The Pandemic, Southern Urbanisms and Collective Live," *Society and Space*, August 3, 2020, www.societyandspace.org/articles/the-pandemic-southern-urbanisms-and-collective-life?fbclid=IwAR1ba5lM3u3TnxrA4bpA-ws3pQg8rO1qAZmPNzuQrF0jh65_jypSkMYIOyo

29 Phil Hubbard, "Law, Pliability and Differential Rights to the City: Legal Geographies of Resistance at the Gentrification Frontier," conference paper [Washington DC: American Association of Geographers Annual Meeting, 2019].

CO-DESIGN AS ENGAGEMENT WITH THE CITY:

RUJAK CENTER FOR URBAN STUDIES, JAKARTA

ELISA SUTANUDJAJA

I am the founder and executive director at the Rujak Center for Urban Studies, a non-profit think-act tank promoting coproduction of knowledge and sustainable urban-regional development in Jakarta. I am an architect with a masters in sustainable and urban development and have taught in various universities since 2006. I have received various awards, including the Education in Sustainable Development JENESYS fellowship from the Government of Japan in 2010, and the Eisenhower Fellowship in 2013.

ABDOUMALIQ SIMONE

I am a Senior Professorial Fellow at the Urban Institute, University of Sheffield, and Visiting Professor of Urban Studies at the African Center for Cities, University of Cape Town. I have worked for a wide range of multilateral institutions and NGOs specializing in urban development, and held academic appointments at Medgar Evers College, the University of Khartoum, Cape Coast University, Witwatersrand University, the New School, and Goldsmiths College. For decades I have traveled across the world working with various municipalities, research groups, and social movements on issues of urban transformation.

Elisa Sutanudjaja: Maliq and I have prepared a question-and-answer session in which Maliq will ask some questions and I will answer.

AbdouMaliq Simone: The first question is since the formal end of authoritarian rule in Indonesia some 33 years ago, the politics of the urban poor and working class have assumed different emphases and different acts of engagement ranging from the politics of recognition to one of co-production with municipal authorities. Could you discuss the critical factors that informed these shifts? Whether it has been the key attainments and challenges entailed by them but particularly for territories where the divisions between public and private household and community are often ambiguous or weakly bounded? What kinds of local and political mechanisms are most effective in making the most of these recent processes of collaborative work with metropolitan government?

Elisa Sutanudjaja: I will start a little bit with a brief introduction about myself. The Rujak Center for Urban Studies is based here in Jakarta. We are a team focusing on the issues of economic sustainability, and we always work together with communities and believe in co-production of practice. Our focuses include housing issues, mobility issues, water and air pollution, and the informal economy. I'm fortunate enough to actively participate in urban struggles. The first observation that has affected our activities quite a bit to us is external, which is a series of evictions during a short period of time, including forced evictions that have become so banal that it's frightening. Externally, we also saw better transparency coming from the local government, which is ironic especially about things like building permits because of the regulations that sometimes contradict the actions that the government is taking. An internal factor is within urban organizations such as ours. The first thing they try to find is new friends and new alliances and new networks, especially with journalists, architects, legal aid organizations, and even sometimes with politicians. Some of them turn to religious organizations as well, and it leads them to working together for better and fairer collaborations on social justice issues.

At the same time, through these processes, the urban poor become more informed and activists for the urban poor also gain new knowledge about what happened and obtain better perspectives. They also learn from the past failures, so it's changed how we operate together as a network and at the same time it's a manifestation of solidarity. For example, within two years there were 305 forced evictions all over the city of Jakarta. Sometimes all of them are enforced with force, with the military and sometimes there are fires that are lit. The last thing is about learning and unlearning from our past mistakes. We know that our government doesn't have enough capability to organize participatory planning as well as to be vigilant due to a lack of trust in the government. We often decide to design ourselves and then the government joins us at the end of the process. The funny thing is that the government actually recognized our efforts as independent community planning, but the governor attended our event and then the provincial government branded it as their event.

AbdouMaliq Simone: Why do places like *kampungs* (i.e., a traditional village or informal settlement within a city) assume such importance in the activist imagination given the diversity of Jakarta and the wide-ranging dynamics of its poor and working-class districts? When we talk about engaging the city in all its diversities, how might a multiplicity of styles be developed that are relevant for places of different histories, ways of exercising authority, and different styles of collective life?

Elisa Sutanudjaja: I view places like leftover places, coastal lines, and riverbanks as problematic places. I cannot really answer the reason why activists like Jakarta Legal Aid operate heavily in these places. Perhaps, since they are a legal aid organization, they mainly work with the urban poor and people who live in disadvantaged areas. For me, it could be the place where there is the potential for restoration. I'm not only an activist, but also a person who always tries to find knew understandings in order to find something new to learn. The degree of complexity presented by a place is not only as a space of restoration but also where the built environment neglects the environmental issues and the nature environment at the same time. If we can work together in

Figure 2.1
Violent government evictions of low-income settlements in Jakarta. Source: Rujak Center for Urban Studies.

such challenging places, it will be easier next time either in South Jakarta or other parts of the city.

AbdouMaliq Simone: Your sense is that the places themselves tell their own story and there are so many different stories that get told by these places. What kind of stories lure, attract, open up, and engage particular kinds of affiliations and particular kinds of possibilities in professional and activist imaginations? For example, the Rujak Center for Urban Studies, which you direct, has long embodied a multipronged approach to urban engagement. You provide technical assistance to community organizations. You conduct public education programs on specific issues. You act as an advocacy group for specific policy changes. You develop detailed annotated maps and case studies of changes in built environments and social compositions. You work closely with municipal and civil society, institutions, and specific projects. And

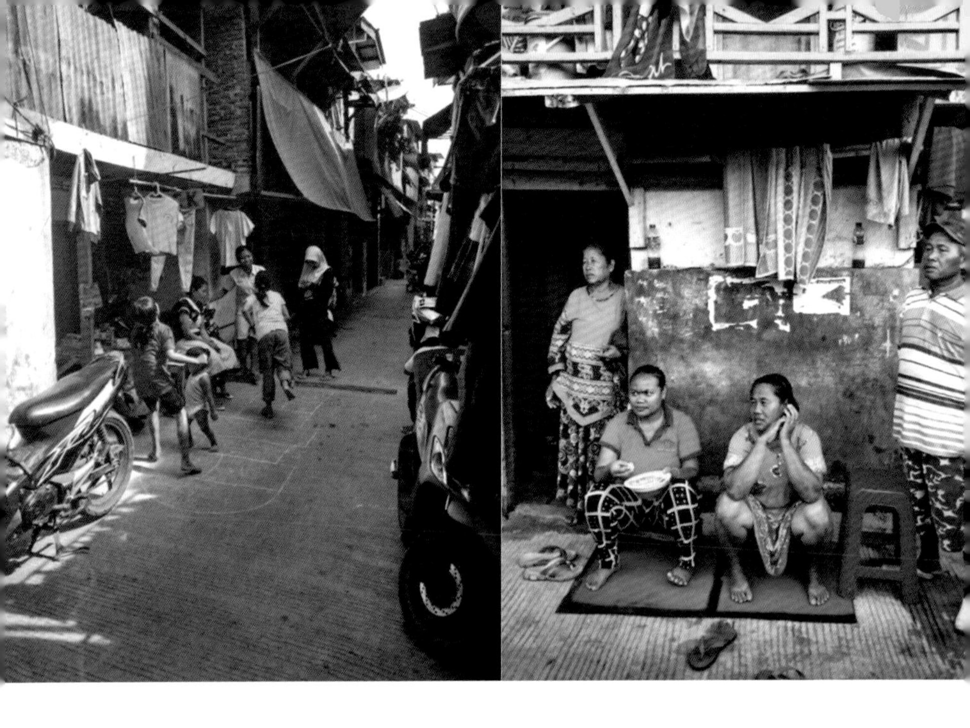

Figure 2.2
Example of a kampung and kampung social life in Jakarta. Source: Rujak Center for Urban Studies.

you have even initiated a wide range of various cultural arts activities. As forms of engagement, how do you see the synergies amongst these different kinds of activities? Moving from the form of the city to other forms of the urban that are yet to take definitive shape, what kinds of engagements can you imagine for these new types of urban territories?

Elisa Sutanudjaja: I'm going to answer the last part of the question, then I will come back to the first part of the question. You see that Jakarta is only this small but then the agglomeration is just like three times of Jakarta and even going further, 120 kilometers to the south. What happens in Jakarta always affects outlying areas. What happens in the hinterland, like a healthy rain season, always affects Jakarta. For people who live outside Jakarta, they have a bit of experience living or even having an activity inside the city.

We believe a city is like a network of information where the citizen is actually the backbone of the infrastructure of knowledge. What we do is connect citizens who live in different areas to let them learn from each other, argue with each other, share their problems, and ask other people from different cities to help them solve their problems. It becomes a unifying network that represents what we believe. We are all in this together, whether it's about mobility, affordable housing, or air pollution. For example, since 2018, I was part of a group of citizens who sued the national government and provincial government about air pollution in Jakarta. As part of this group of plaintiffs, there were 22 people out of 32 total who were from outside Jakarta, living in neighboring cities. This was an act of solidarity because what happens in Jakarta could affect them.

Question: Elisa, you said something quite remarkable in the first part of your presentation about unlearning and learning when it comes to political contracts. Is that something that is the ethos of your organization, the Rujak

Figure 2.3
Example of collective and collaborative efforts.
Source: Rujak Center for Urban Studies.

Center, or does it emerge out of particular projects? Can you talk a little bit more about this, how it happens, the learning and unlearning?

Elisa Sutanudjaja: The political contract is a typical mode of operation done by the Urban Poor Consortium, which is a national organization with a focus mostly on the urban poor and the informal sector. Rujak was involved in two political contracts alongside them, one in 2012 and the other in 2017. We thought that the 2012 contract would be easier to understand and to be implemented by the government. If the content of the contract is simple, such as something general like better public participation, then it can easily be translated into a different set of rules. But then the government didn't follow any of that and we also learned it's difficult to apply. That was a process of unlearning because we thought it would be easier if the contract can be understood by the public, but then it turned out to be difficult to implement. Then, in the second political contract in 2017, we did a very detailed contract containing 30 pages focusing on issues such as, "What are the demands of the citizens and what are the demands of the specific *kampungs*?" There are 25 *kampungs*, so you write the contract specifically based on their needs and negotiate one by one with each *kampung*. The negotiations were with lawyers, including possibilities for litigation as well as dealing with political issues. Apparently, those kinds of contracts are in fact

Figure 2.4
Jakarta is a large agglomeration with a vast hinterland, including large infrastructure networks and vast bodies of water.
Source: Rujak Center for Urban Studies.

easier to implement, so this is part of the learning process for us. The provincial governor wanted to implement the contract, but apparently, he could not do that because one cannot pursue a discriminatory policy that only applies to specific *kampungs*, and so he had to make a city-wide policy based on the contract, which was our aim in the beginning. That's another part of the learning process for us, in which the real victory was when he decided to do city-wide community planning instead of only for 25 *kampungs*.

Question: How do citizens of Jakarta relate to issues of climate change in Jakarta?

Elisa Sutanudjaja: You cannot really say "climate change" if you have conversations with specific populations in Jakarta. You have to change the term of climate change into different terms. For example, if you have a conversation with *kampung* residents, they will have no idea what climate change is, but they will have an idea about why the rain is more severe and more frequent than before and why the flood is increasing. Then they will have full engagement in such a discussion. But if you suddenly come and ask, what do you think about climate change, I don't think they will bite, or they will answer anything about that, or even know what you were talking about. So it really depends on who is the audience and where they live. If you live in the coastal area then you answer the question about the wind or about the rain, but if you live in the residential complex then ask about the quality of water because it's related and because the water is coming from far away: "Why is the quality getting worse and worse?"

AbdouMaliq Simone: It's difficult to say that anything like climate change actually exists as some kind of univocal phenomenon. I mean it is a multiplicity of different kinds of processes that are intersected and experienced by different populations in different ways, and I think that the abstraction of climate change just doesn't have very much resonance in terms of the way in which many inhabitants experience the changes that they do recognize and that have substantial implications for them.

Question: I am curious about the process of community-action planning as you presented early on. To what extent did the community planning process reach its consensus?

Elisa Sutanudjaja: There are different types of involvement in different matters. For example, in one *kampung*, there were 241 families, and it would be complicated to have 241 families in all participatory planning processes. The way it usually works is that you always have to prepare before you start the formal community planning process. First you have to make sure that you have a team within themselves and that they choose their own team. Then, they do community mapping together as a team, and we as community organizers do it together with them doing

Figure 2.5 Community involvement takes many different guises, such as this smaller-scale workshop with local residents. Source: Rujak Center for Urban Studies.

rapid assessment procedures, also called RAP. Then we train the *kampung* team about specific issues like building regulations or zoning laws or cooperatives. For example, one of the most significant achievements was when the *kampung* team managed to argue with the government about specific activities that can't be allowed in that area. The mothers in the *kampung* proposed to set up a community kindergarten but the local government officials said no. However, they managed to access a provincial Jakarta website and showed that this is actually allowed in this area because the zoning says so. So the local government officials didn't know but the mothers knew, which I think was one of the proudest moments for me because they managed to argue about a specific case. After the training, they have community-based activities, such as a series of meetings based on the analysis to reconstruct the history together. In this process, there are larger meetings and when we do the work plan, the *kampung* team works together with us at Rujak. From that we come up with design guidelines and subsequently the architects in Rujak, and sometimes the residents themselves also make models, to show what they really want. Then we come up with an architectural design and proposal for the government.

Question: Are there areas of expertise or skill that your organization would want to connect more to? This could be additional expertise or skill that Rujak may not have now but it would be beneficial if you connected more to those.

Elisa Sutanudjaja: It would be very nice if we can have more connection with economists or people who understand financial accounting. Because when we are doing a lot of research about issues such as land that is owned by the developers, one has to read a lot of financial statements and to understand the details because the difference is often in the details, such as who owns which assets (e.g., land and buildings) and how they operate.

PUBLIC REALM ETHNOGRAPHY:

UNDERSTANDING AND STUDYING THE PUBLIC REALM

ALASDAIR JONES

I am a Senior Lecturer in the Department of Geography at the University of Exeter. I am an interdisciplinary social scientist with expertise in the fields of urban studies, including sustainable urbanism, and program evaluation. My research aims to use, refine, and develop empirical approaches that enable the generation of insights into critical questions concerning urban planning, urban public space, and public policy programs.

Alasdair Jones: For this talk, I want to think about ways we might ethnographically study public realm settings, which we can think about as a particular typology of social setting in cities. Empirically, my work builds on an ethnographic study of London's South Bank, which is a riverside public space next to a set of arts institutions in central London. I conducted a four-year ethnographic study of this space, and I was interested in its production and reproduction, its formal production and informal production, its regulation, and its use as a public space. After that study, I've developed various themes including an interest in play in public space, in the curation of public space, in the distinction between the everyday and the exceptional in public realm settings.

I would argue that public realm ethnography is a kind of interdisciplinary process. You're interested in social relationships but also in the spatial constitution of those, and in the social constitution of space. This is the kind of dialectical idea that Henri Lefebvre articulates well and that is evident in studies characterized by greater attention to the relationship between the social and spatial dimensions of the setting under study. This is how I think about public realm ethnographies. I would say what a public realm ethnography is trying to do is a form, spatio-analysis, as Ed Soja defined it, or the analysis of the social production of social space.

Participant observation in the public realm is particularly challenging, I argue. Participant observation is a method in which a researcher takes part in the daily activities, rituals, interactions, and events of a group of people, as a means to learn the explicit and tacit aspects of their life routines and cultures. In the public realm however, social relations are characterized by a variegated space-time of aggregation. There's likely to be multiple groups, not to mention individuals. They are co-present at any given time and using the space over time. Social phenomena, activities, rituals, interactions, and so on, in which a researcher might participate, are definitively heterogeneous and fleeting. You can't participate in all of these things at the same time.

The methodological questions this poses are, "What activities or what groups can, or should, the ethnographer participate in during their field work? How can a deep understanding of the cultural significance of social activities be generated if practitioners are transient and the activities are fleeting? How can we understand the experience, value, meaningfulness of being in the public realm?" And finally, "How can a fieldworker meaningfully participate in being alone in public?"

My interest as a methodologist is in how public realm ethnographies are methodologically carried out. I'm interested in the things that public realm ethnographies find, but I'm particularly interested in how they're actually done. This interest supplements reflections on my own research experience, with a review of accounts of in-situ fieldwork in similar sorts of studies. These are studies that share an assumption that space is socially constructed as well as materially embodied. These studies have a mutual interest in empirically exploring how urban public space is experienced and rendered meaningful by users. They're interested in exploring how such space is produced and produced as public, not only formally through its design, planning, and management, but also

Figure 3.1
London Southbank Centre Graffiti.
Source: Alasdair Jones (photo taken: 23rd August 2013).

through its everyday use or social practice. One of the features of these studies is that they're often mixed-method approaches, combining different sorts of data collection and analysis, to approximate an ethnographic study.

What are some of the things we can draw out from public realm ethnographies through reflecting on some of their principles? I've got four here.

First, public realm ethnographies are characterized by the primacy of the visual, the predominance of non-participant observational data collection. Secondly, observational data collection tends to be sequential and iterative, characterized by a shift in focus from the macro to the micro, and from fixed to flexible. We're moving between different modes of data collection. Thirdly, research is characterized by a combination of systematic, non-participant observation of research at defined spatial zones (such as intensive observation of particular social phenomena) and an itinerant mode of ethnographic being or hanging out in public space. If I was to come up with a term that's the equivalent of participant observation in public realm ethnography, it would be the idea of, (co-)present cognition, in which data is collected using field notes and field diaries through an emphasis on physical co-presence in the field, and through the markedly reflexive multisensorial and perambulatory, or walking-based recording of data. Fourth, public realm ethnographers supplement their observational data with the collection of typically short intercept interviews with others co-present in the public realm setting. We can expect to have shorter interactions with people, rather than lengthy talks with them.

The public realm does have exceptional moments where it has incredibly powerful repercussions for society, but at the same time it has a kind of everyday meaningfulness that we should be attentive to as well. In terms of the former, we might ask why are some spaces more amenable to activists and exceptional events than others? My sense is that in the case of the Southbank Centre in London, it has been a site of various forms of protest in the past because it was an arts institution, it has a visual arts gallery, a music space, a concert hall, theater, and is open to other imaginations (including regarding the ways that public realm can be used).

That may be a very niche example, but it offers one possible explanation for why some spaces are more amenable to activists than others. In order to identify and understand such exceptional examples of public realm, we have to address questions such as, "How is that space constituted? What sort of area is it in? What sorts of institutions surround that space? And what does that mean for how the space is perceived by the public, but also perceived by those formally responsible for the management of that space?" For example, one of my opinions is that the ownership of a space does not necessarily designate that space as public realm or private realm. It's actually, in some ways, the use of the space that we should be attentive to.

CO-DESIGN AS LONG-TERM PROCESS:

HASIRU DALA, BENGALURU

NALINI SHEKAR

My name is Nalini Shekar, and I co-founded Hasiru Dala, which means "green force" in the regional Kannada language, and which is an organization that works with the waste pickers primarily in Bengaluru, India. Waste pickers are people who pick up recyclables on the street, which is what we throw as waste, and with their labor they sort, grade, and make it into a tradable commodity. Our main objectives at Hasiru Dala are to provide space for these workers within the formal solid-waste management system of the city by working with wastepickers who are part of the informal sector and to promote appropriate, decentralized, and cost-effective solutions for solid-waste management and decent livelihoods.

NEHA SAMI

I am Neha Sami and I am currently faculty at the Indian Institute for Human Settlements in Bangalore, India, where I teach on questions of governance and sustainability and anchor the Research Program. My research focuses on the governance of infrastructure, especially mega-infrastructure in the context of post-liberalization urban India. I also work on questions of environmental governance particularly at the sub-national scale, focusing on institutional analysis and state capacity. I am a corresponding editor for the International Journal of Urban and Regional Research, and have served on the editorial collective of Urbanization.

Nalini Shekar: There is a huge perception in India that waste pickers are dirty, and that they don't know anything. They are not educated. We are changing that perception to acknowledge that they're in fact semi-skilled workers and that they know more than you and me about waste material in order to make it into a tradable commodity and raw material for the recycling industry. We don't call them waste pickers; we call them robust entrepreneurs and silent environmentalists. And we consider their views to be design tools to move forward and make changes. We aim to do this through both research and implementation. Research is always important: through our analysis, we showed that the city of Bengaluru is saving almost 8.2 million Indian rupees from its municipal budget because of the informal work that waste pickers do through the collection and transportation of recyclable materials that are recovered from municipal solid waste.

One of the things that we at Hasiru Dala were able to demonstrate early on was the establishment of Dry Waste Collection Centers as decentralized infrastructure for waste collection and sorting. These are places where inorganic waste like paper, plastic, cloth, metal, and glass are aggregated for the formal collection system. These Centers are run by waste pickers who are otherwise not integrated in the formal system. It is also important for Dry Waste Collection Centers to look aesthetically attractive as well as functional, particularly given the assumption around waste management and waste picking being 'dirty' or 'unclean' work. We used a mural to paint portraits at these Centers of the people who work there. We are also working on educating citizens through awareness building among the wider public about waste pickers and the critical service they perform for the city.

Another important aspect of our work at Hasiru Dala is to negotiate with the municipal government of Bengaluru in ways that are helpful to waste pickers as well as citizens. We have created a range of spaces for waste pickers to contribute through dialogue with multiple stakeholders as well as petition for their rights to the judiciary and the court system. For example, in 2011 when we asked the local commissioner for decentralized infrastructure

Figure 4.1
Dry Waste Collection Center painted in a colorful pattern.
Source: Hasiru Dala.

for inorganic waste management, he said "Bengaluru is such a big city, how can we allocate space for Dry Waste Collection Centers in every administrative ward?" However, through constant dialogue and negotiation, we have now created 166 Dry Waste Collection Centers throughout the city. This space is given by the city to the poor to provide their utility services and it has taken about 10 years to create these physical spaces. The bylaws of the city have been amended to now say that all the dry and inorganic waste will be collected only by waste pickers or a small women's collective. We have managed to change the policies. All this happened because citizens demanded it. We partnered with citizens to demonstrate how waste pickers were beneficial to sustainable waste management and to streamline collection services, and those efforts helped make it happen.

Waste pickers and their work are often invisible and unacknowledged. An important part of our mission at Hasiru Dala is to change this. In addition to pushing for policy changes, we are also aiming to make this work more visible in public spaces around the city. One illustration of this is a recently completed mural on

you are for us
we are
you for
BBMP

one of the walls of one of Bengaluru's prominent iconic public buildings. Located along a major thoroughfare in Bengaluru, the Utility Building had become a place where garbage was dumped. The mural is a painted portrait of one waste picker and one sanitation worker that depicts the interconnectedness of informal and formal waste sectors and "essential workers" engaged in it. We cleaned it up and we engaged with a lot of people who came, stood, watched, and asked us, "What is this? Why are you doing it?" In the process, many of them participated, including upper- and middle-class citizens alongside waste pickers. There was lot of discussion that happened during that phase. These are some of the types of things that we have done in the public realm.

Neha Sami: The thing that's interesting about the work that Hasiru Dala does is that they take something like waste, which is an output of our shared urban life, and they have found a way of making it visible and of making the people who do that work visible as well. The way in which the Dry Waste Collection Centers have been developed and the way in which the ownership of the process of managing and collecting the waste has been transferred over to the people who do the work has gone a long way in helping them feel empowered. Hasiru Dala has now gone from being present only in Bengaluru to working across southern India, which is a huge achievement in the last decade for a community-based organization.

Another thing that I also want to highlight is the importance of designing collectively and the time that it takes. The temporal aspect of co-designing the physical spaces but also the time that it takes to build trust within government, the time it takes to build these alliances across multiple stakeholders and players within a city, then beyond the city to take that to other locations, and to continue to use the same philosophy. It allows us to rethink

Figure 4.2
Mural of a waste picker and a sanitation worker on the side of the Utility Building on a major thoroughfare in Bengaluru.
Source: Hasiru Dala, 2021.

the idea of public realm as not just something that's a physical, tangible space but also something that's an ongoing process, as well as opening these processes up much more collectively to broader groups of people.

Question: I'm really glad Neha brought up the question of time. Can you take us through how Hasiru Dala started and what was your original intention? The second question is specifically dealing with the relationship between social stigma of waste pickers and the time it really takes, in your experience, to challenge such a social stigma?

Nalini Shekar: I moved to Bengaluru in 2010, when there was lot of discussion by middle-class environmentalists about sustainable waste management. They were all very well-meaning people but there was no discussion about waste pickers who were entirely absent from the process. So, we did a study that showed 35,000 waste pickers were there in Bengaluru. How can you not recognize them? That is why immediately we started organizing them on the ground. At the same time, we went to the court, which is called the Lok Adalat and is an alternative dispute resolution system within the High Court where they bring all the parties together to negotiate, discuss, and find a way forward. They brought in the state government, they brought in the local government, they brought in the citizens, and we represented the waste pickers. We were not well organized at the time but we started to show them how much money is being saved through the informal work of the waste pickers for the city. Then, I said, "You have to recognize their historical contribution and you have to start by giving them occupational identity cards." When we started in 2010, it was not very clear who the waste belonged to that was on the street. When the waste pickers used to pick it up, they used to be shouted at by the local government officials. They would be shouted at by citizens. They were harassed by the police. The occupational identity card, that we helped to obtain, said they had a right to collect waste on the street within the jurisdiction of Bengaluru, which was a big achievement for us. Now, it has become a law across the nation. So, that's how we started very small, and we grew organically, but our vision was big.

Question: Could you talk a little about the way in which the waste collection workers were convened around your initiative, and how you helped them to understand the need for–and meaning of–such work? How was trust built? What were the mechanisms for communication, interaction at the very basic community level?

Nalini Shekar: This is an interesting question, because I have done this from ground up in the Indian cities of Pune and Bengaluru. It's a similar story. For example, I remember one of my colleagues who came and said, "These two women, whenever I go to talk to them, they go and hide in the rainwater drains." Because they don't see you around normally and because they don't want to believe you since there have been so many people who have already been cheated when somebody tells them, to the effect, "Okay, give me money and I'll get you this social benefit." And so, it was difficult but going in again and again to meet them is the best thing for building trust over time. Then, when the government said they would give an occupational identity card to the waste pickers, it became an extremely good vehicle for us to build upon. Persistence is the only way and once they begin to trust you, then you have won the war. Now, we hear from people in different cities, "We have heard that you guys work with waste pickers; why don't you come to our city?"

Question: Neha, could I ask you to speak a little bit more about the way your research and teaching institution, the Indian Institute of Human Settlements, has been working with Hasiru Dala, and what are your future projects with them?

Neha Sami: Before that, I just want to add that everything that Nalini's been saying demonstrates the temporal aspect of designing collectively. I think that it's something that we often disregard, partly because we want quick solutions. We often ignore the amount of effort and time that goes into not only building but also sustaining long-standing embedded solutions. As Nalini was saying, it is a constant struggle of keeping at it.

One of the things that Nalini mentioned earlier today is to find ways in which waste-picker communities can express themselves in multiple formats, and the murals that you saw were one aspect of it. Now we're trying to find ways in which we can help and train around issues of writing and communication. We're trying to find ways in which we can conduct workshops that would allow us to train and facilitate capacity building within the community to be able to be their own voice in terms of writing. A lot of people have written case study analyses about them by coming and doing research on them, including our institute. But the community itself has not been able to find a way of speaking. So, we're hoping to start with both Kannada (the native language of the state of Karnataka, where Bengaluru is situated) and English, with Kannada as the language that they're most familiar with. We would like to find different ways of incrementally continuing to support the work that they do.

We also have several of our current and former students who work with Hasiru Dala in various capacities. Over the years, we have also brought the team from Hasiru Dala into our classroom and teaching spaces in an attempt to broaden the kinds of knowledge that get transacted in such spaces as well as broaden the notion of who counts as 'faculty.'

The case study analysis that we (i.e., Indian Institute of Human Settlements) researched and prepared about the work of Hasiru Dala was used to train not only the Indian Administrative Service, which is the elite civil service of the national government of India, but also for state and municipal governments. We're trying to provide knowledge on the other side of things to show it as a kind of demonstration project where potential bureaucrats can

Figure 4.3
Hasiru Dala works collectively through alliances with multiple stakeholders, including the local government.
Source: Hasiru Dala, 2021.

take into their own practices and their own cities.

Question: Are there global forums or platforms for different approaches to waste picking? This activity exists globally in various ways, and I wonder if such a network would be useful, if it doesn't already exist?

Nalini Shekar: It already exists. Our different groups have all come together to create a network called the Global Alliance of Waste Pickers. There are differences because the laws of each country are different, but there are some common principles and actions we can work on together, such as member-based organizations and ways of working with different kinds of private waste management companies. [Editor: For more information on the Global Alliance of Waste Pickers, please visit their website: https://globalrec.org/]

CO-DESIGN AS CONTESTATION OF POWER:

UNIÃO NACIONAL POR MORADIA POPULAR, SÃO PAULO

EVANIZA RODRIGUES

I'm a social worker with a master's in architecture and urbanism. I work in the elaboration and management of urban- and housing-policy proposals in popular movements and the training of social stakeholders. I work with self-managed housing programs, and I am the executive coordinator of the União Nacional por Moradia Popular. I was chief of staff at the Secretariat of Urban Programs of the Ministry of Cities and advisor to the presidency of Caixa Econômica Federal.

FERNANDO LARA

I work on theorizing spaces of the Americas with emphasis on the dissemination of architecture and planning ideas beyond the traditional disciplinary boundaries. In my several articles, I have discussed the modern and the contemporary architecture of our continent, its meaning, context, and social-economic insertion. My latest publications include Excepcionalidad del Modernismo Brasileño, Modern Architecture in Latin America, and Quid Novi. I hold the Roessner Centennial Professorship at the University of Texas at Austin where I currently serve as Director of the PhD Program in Architecture.

INTRODUCTION

The National Union for Popular Housing (União Nacional por Moradia Popular) is a popular movement organization in Brazil that has been fighting for 30 years and has acted within the main governmental programs on urban development at the Council of Society and various other instances. As Brazil is a federal country, its housing policies are developed at three levels: at the municipal, state, and federal levels.

CO-DESIGN AS A CHALLENGE TO POWER STRUCTURES

Our topic at the symposium addresses co-design as a challenge to power structures. That is, how from popular movement and grassroots organizations, we can challenge, contest, and contribute to the transformation of existing power structures, especially structures that are exclusionary and elitist.

Evaniza Rodrígues: Here it is important to think in different yet equally important dimensions. The first is the form of interventions

that build social fabric. We know that the strengthening of organizations comes from the people, from people's territorial settings, and from their interests. From there we can organize ourselves and develop proposals to assert those rights that are denied to us. We must recognize that these processes are always long because we first have to understand our situation as a collective situation, meaning that the problem affects me as well as the person next to me, my neighbor. In addition, these processes are generally very complex because they involve compounding and often clashing interests. For example, in one occupation that took place where we had many undocumented immigrants, they were afraid both of being evicted and of being regularized, as this implied the risk of being discovered as undocumented and being expelled from the country.

Figure 5.1
Process of the Social Construction of Urban Habitat. Source: Henrique Geddo.

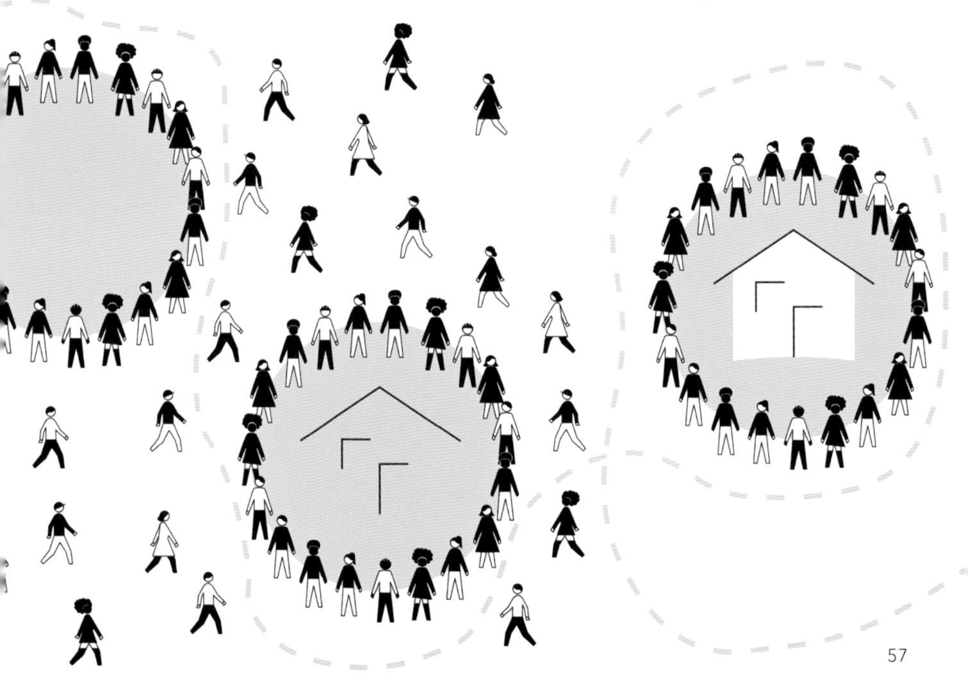

This is why grassroots organizing and day-to-day organizing is so important. It allows people with common interests to recognize each other and start to act collectively. Grassroots pressure is the tool we use the most. When we take over a building, or a plot of land, or fight against eviction (which is one way for governments to put pressure on us), we become seen. Because if homeless people stay where they are, be it in their spot, tent, or land, they become invisible. Society does not understand them, does not recognize them, and does not see their needs, their priorities.

On the other hand, we also understand the importance of institutional engagement. In Brazil over the last 30 years, we have tried to develop formal advocacy spaces in local councils, especially in the city of São Paulo, so that the authorities recognize the different sectors of society and their right to decide, to be involved in decision-making processes. We cannot exclude the state because it is the entity levying and collecting taxes, even if such actions benefit the interests of the privileged few more than the interests of people in the margins. However, we can fight so that the state redistributes wealth.

Another important aspect is networking. We understand that as important as local territorial action is, it is also necessary to create networks amongst social movements, with academia and non-governmental organizations, with other friends and in other countries. The Co-Designing Publics network set up here is an example of how people with different points of view can contribute to the development of policies, strategies, and different visions against issues afflicting people. Here is where universities can facilitate knowledge exchange deriving from academia and from different social organizations, groups, and people in the margins.

An important topic for us is awareness raising as well as denouncement because many of society's problems are only seen by those who suffer them. This is why, for example, we have painted unoccupied properties, to show the existence of unoccupied properties in the city whilst we have many homeless people around. It is also a way of showing society that it is necessary to make changes, investment, and public policies to address such situations. Otherwise, if we do not make such matters visible, we normalize settings that are not normal such as people living in *favelas* (i.e., low-income settlements that can be concentrations of poverty along with inadequate infrastructure, but not in every case), people living without water, and everyday evictions. It is important to showcase such problems to the whole of society either through traditional media or alternative platforms such as social media, so that we can also present our point of view on these issues. Empowering people also seems crucial to us. We know that formal education is still exclusive and fails to address issues that are often important for society.

Finally, we also understand that people can put public policies into practice. We see processes of policy self-management through which organized people manage public resources, budgets, land, and projects to solve their problems. It is not about destroying the state, but about creating groups recognized by governments that can implement policies and put them into action. But there is much work to be done as part of a long-term strategy that creates accumulations of gains and lessons from other joint processes.

PROJECT, ABSTRACTION, AND CO-DESIGN

Fernando Lara: To talk about co-design in the context of Brazil we must start by reflecting on the concept of 'project,' something that can be very specific to architecture. We must remember that in Latin languages, the word 'project' that we use comes from the Latin *proiectare*, which means to cast your eyes into the future. That is to visualize, to make plans, and to promote a future. So, we start from the idea of project, which is to abet a future

UNIÃO
MORADIA POPULAR
CMP
CMP
ENQUANTO MORAR FOR UM PRIVILÉGIO, OCUPAR É UM DIREITO
UNIÃO
NACIONAL POR
MORADIA POPULAR
JORNADA NACIONAL DE LUTA EM DEFESA DA REFORMA URBANA
CMP
UNIÃ
NACIONAL PO
MORADIA
POPULAR
UNIÃO
MORADIA POPULAR

within the traditional idea of design. Then comes the question: What kind of future do we want to promote and what kind of inequalities are manifested when designing? Here it is important to highlight that planning, as projection, is also a process that excludes those whose basic needs are lacking. It is very difficult to project and to be able to think about future goals when the most immediate problem is obtaining food for today. That is why the struggle is often for the minimum, so that injustice is at least recognized. There is no possibility of a future that is abstract or a project for those who have enormous shortages today such as the reality of hunger.

Abstraction in the idea of the project about the future is fundamental. This is not a problem per se, but its instrumental use in history to control and organize territory based on geometric and mathematical concepts and to generate development, must be acknowledged. As Arturo Escobar reminds us, the problem is that there is no modernization without colonization. All the positive developments of modernization have been built at the expense of many people who suffer from the processes of colonization: people who do not have access to vaccines, people who do not have access to clean water, people who do not have access to resources.

This is precisely why co-design is so important, and why it is important to approach it from the perspective of thinkers from the global south. For

Figure 5.2
Occupation of a building in Sao Paulo by União Nacional por Moradia Popular.
Source: Evaniza Rodrigues, 2009.

instance, Paulo Freire worked on a counter-hegemonic theory that does not rule out abstraction. The process of teaching to read requires abstraction: it is essential that the person learning to read learns to abstract sounds from a text, and learns to translate these sounds into letters, into words, and thus to form language structures. The question is how to remove the privilege of abstraction. Freire proposes ways to dismantle the privilege of any language, and it is interesting to think about how to apply this to co-design processes. What would a process that could dismantle the privilege of urban design and architectural design look like? Freire dismantles a power structure instilled in language to empower the poorest to control their own narrative. We must do the same in the way we intervene in spaces. Here the idea of co-design is central, to start thinking about ways of building a city with more justice and equality. In this respect, the work of housing movements in Brazil is key since they directly confront the structures of capitalist power that dominate an entire urban narrative; one in which those who fight for their housing are 'irregulars,' and do not conform to the law. This narrative is strong and movements such as the National Union for Popular Housing in São Paulo are at the forefront when revealing the injustices, asymmetries, and inequalities of city-building processes.

Question: In your experience, what is the role of practitioners and academics of the built environment disciplines: architects, landscape architects, designers, city planners, etc. to effectively challenge the power structure?

Evaniza Rodrigues: First, I think that the university must stop being the exclusive space of higher-income sectors. Here in Brazil, for example, the university was basically just for students from the middle- or upper-middle-income and white-collar-income sectors. Public policies were able to encourage students from other walks of society to enter university for the first time. And it is not only about access, but also about bringing about changes in the content that academia produces. So, when a homeless family, with a homeless youth, when a young person from the favela enters university, it is not only to learn information already elaborated, but also to generate other knowledge that may not already exist. The other thing is to create opportunities for the exchange of academic knowledge with the knowledge coproduced by organizations, people in the margins, and other groups of people. When we do this, these things intertwine and can produce new things, and even re-orient academic disciples.

Fernando Lara: I am somewhat optimistic about the university. There are people in universities all over the world who want to change things, who want to do things differently, who want to think of ways to implement other futures. But the academic world is also a closed system that self-protects and self-regulates. Like all large institutions, universities change very slowly. It seems to me that the important thing is to locate and amplify the voices that are thinking important and new things.

Another central element is not to let the voices of the global south be appropriated and distorted (or even be manipulated) by the institutions of the global north. Protecting the authenticity of ideas from the global south is very important. For instance, universities as systems are not ready to do this; they are not ready to recognize knowledge from the Amazon, India, or from parts of Africa. You must open these spaces, amplify these voices, and be very critical of voices from the global north who regularly appropriate ideas like Paulo Freire's to keep the status quo as it is.

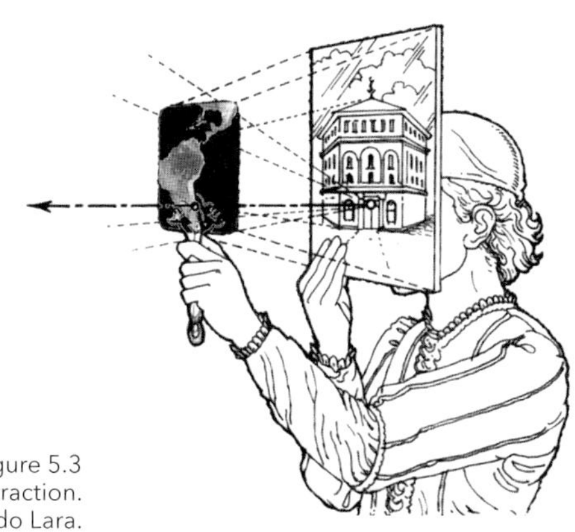

Figure 5.3
Abstraction.
Source: Fernando Lara.

WHO REALLY DESIGNS?

MARIANELA D'APRILE

I'm an architecture writer. I've also been a union organizer, and I did spend the last three years on the national leadership of the Democratic Socialists of America, which is the largest socialist organization in the US in almost 100 years, with about 95,000 members now and chapters in 200 cities across the country. And so my work concerns the political agency of architecture and architects, or really the lack thereof, and in particular I'm interested in looking at how architecture and politics intersect and the motivating factors that shape our built environment.

Marianela D'Aprile: The story of the Thompson Center in downtown Chicago, which is a federal building that was completed in the 1980s, lays bare who has power over our shared public space and really who controls what gets built and ultimately who gets to use the things that get built.

The Thompson Center was publicly commissioned by the state of Illinois in the early 1980s to house state government offices and other public services, as well as a public indoor plaza and food court. Construction of the Helmut Jahn-designed building was completed in 1985. After many years of neglect, in particular of its glass exterior which caused overheating in summer and overcooling in winter, maintenance costs became too high for the state to bear. Illinois governor J.B. Pritzker put the building up for sale in 2021, risking its demolition. Since then, the building has been purchased for $70 million by

Prime Group, who does not plan to demolish the building, but its key public spaces will cease to be so, depriving Chicagoans, for example, of one of the few indoor public spaces in a city that's dangerously cold for many months out of the year.

I want to talk a bit about how we change that and shift the balance of who gets to make decisions about our shared public space in our built environment. We can imagine from the example of the Architecture Lobby's campaign called "Not Our Wall" how coordinated action within architecture, alongside construction workers and building-trades workers, could result in both immediate reforms against building things like border walls or against building things like prisons.

In early 2017, the U.S. Department of Homeland Security—at the request of then-President Donald Trump—released a request for proposals for border-wall prototypes to begin the bidding phase of new wall construction on the border with Mexico. The Architecture Lobby led a campaign to get architecture firms to pledge not to participate in this process, successfully getting one of the only three architecture, engineering, and construction firms in the country who could've taken on such a project to rescind their proposal.

And in the long term, we can also imagine how we could use worker power against the interests of developers and in favor of the interests of those who actually use architecture. There's a tremendous amount of solidarity to be built once people organize themselves with other entities that might also be organized, whether that be unions on the ground or community organizations.

Question: What do you think we should do to include more architects, urbanists, and everyone else in this process? And what do you think is the key thing to do in those kinds of conflicted public spaces?

Marianela D'Aprile: I think it does help to have something to organize against or something to organize for. At least in the United States, the building-trades unions are the most conservative unions typically because they are the ones who need big construction companies or real estate developers to make their money, so that the workers themselves can put food on their tables. Their interests are actually linked up with the interests of their bosses in ways that workers in other sectors are not. It's the same thing in many ways, I think, for architects. So, it's very hard to fight for the ideal when actually you don't know if you're going to be able to pay your rent in a given month. At the same time, I think it is our responsibility–those of us who are committed to a long-term fight against capitalism–for people and for workers to take that long view and try to seize any opportunities that we can in order to organize within this long-term perspective.

Question: How do you think empowering architects to think about public spaces will also impact work on climate change? And does this imply the need for political organization and moral stance in architecture corporations or labor unions?

Marianela D'Aprile: I think it's a question of thinking about the built environment as a whole and public space as a common good as

opposed to individual buildings or individual designs. I do think some of that will have to come from political education, but I don't think it's only about changing the minds of individual architects, and I think this gets at the second part of your question. I think there are plenty of architects who think public space is good and necessary and that it should be beautiful. But then obviously that is very hard to carry out when the interests that makes spaces and make built environments possible are usually moneyed interests or for-profit interests. And so I think that, yes, this absolutely does require a kind of political organization, perhaps within the

Figure 6.1
The Thompson Center atrium in Chicago. Source: Kenneth C. Zirkel, 2019, Wikimedia Commons.

profession, to again get architects started thinking about how they act as political actors in the world. And then, how they can perhaps use the tools of their profession to improve certain things. Then, ultimately, a lot of the change that's going to have to happen in regard to the climate crisis, specifically as it pertains to the built environment, will have to come through policy, will have to come through community organization or through political organization.

If what it takes is for architects, first, to develop a professional responsibility or an idea of what they as architects could do to improve things so they can then act in the broader political world, I think that's totally fine. But I think these processes of politicization are stacked onto each other and feed into each other, so we have to start with one first step. First, it's about seeing public spaces as a common good, and then realizing that we have to fight for it, and then knowing that we can't just fight for it as individual architects or individual professionals. We have to do it as political actors in the world.

Question: Do you see this happening through a process of changing in the societal location of the profession of the architects, such as a result of social movements? For example, I can see a link between what's happening in South America now and what's happening in the United States.

Marianela D'Aprile: I do think there's been a bit of change happening, especially in architectural education. I think the best examples are ones that ask students to look at the larger systems that rule our world, and what roles architecture and other designers and the built-environment practitioners play in those larger systems. I do have a reference. Billy Fleming, who has been teaching at the University of Pennsylvania, ran a studio called the Green New Deal Studio over the last year and a half and has recently published a paper on architecture education in this particular political moment, especially as it relates to the climate crisis. It's a really interesting case study of how to conduct design education that is still realistic about the agency of architects and of designers and of buildings, while not abandoning design entirely and still looking at the larger context.

EDITOR'S NOTE:

Building upon Marianela's forward-looking comments, one could add more examples such as the Master's in Design and Urban Ecologies program at the Parsons School of Design of The New School university in New York City, and the Master's Urban Design program at Cardiff University in the United Kingdom—especially its three-year experimental studio in designing critical and transdisciplinary anti-gentrification strategies in the Grangetown area in the city of Cardiff. The editor was deeply involved in both of them. There are other examples around the world, such as the Spatial Practices program at Central Saint Martins in London.

CO-DESIGN AS RESISTANCE:

CAMBODIAN CENTER FOR HUMAN RIGHTS, PHNOM PENH

SOPHEAP CHAK

I'm Sopheap from Cambodia. I work for the Cambodian Center for Human Rights, and we are a human rights organization that works to promote and protect civil and political rights. Mainly, we work on supporting fundamental freedoms, supporting human rights defenders, and a number of issues including the impacts of business interests on human rights. I'm looking forward to further discussing the co-designing of urban publics within the context of our Cambodian case study.

SIMON SPRINGER

I'm Simon Springer, Professor of Human Geography at the University of Newcastle. I am also Director of the Center for Urban and Regional Studies at my university, as well as Head of Discipline for Geography and Environmental Studies. For the last 20 years that I have been doing research in Cambodia that there's been a lot to be critical about, and to be honest, to be quite upset about. And that's what we're going to talk about today.

Simon Springer: In my work, I've essentially considered two sort of competing views of the public. The first one being an ordered view based on ideas like surveillance and stability. If there is an overarching discourse in the context of Cambodia, it is this drive for stability. The government uses this idea in one particular way, in that they're meaning largely economic stability, and the stability of their regime. This is contrasted with the view of the public realm, public space, a space for resistance, for freedom, and for belonging. A space for articulating ideas that are not in keeping with the government's overarching views. This would be a view of the public that is tolerant of the risks of disorder.

In contrast then to this ordered view, the public realm can be seen as forum for all social groups, a place for performance and speech, and the crucible of radical democracy. The Cambodian government looks at contestation or conflict in a very negative sort of connotation. Of course, there's positive things that come out of contestation as well, and that's the view that everyday Cambodians are bringing to the table, in terms of their resistance to various issues that affect their everyday lives.

One of the primary ways that politics are playing out in the Cambodian context is through neoliberalism. The way that the Cambodian government is approaching this is in wanting to create a space that is conducive to international investment, and this idea that Cambodia is open for business, and that this business will flow smoothly within the context of their country. What this leads to though is that the public realm in Cambodia has taken on this sort of Disneyfication of space where things like entertainment, capital, and security take precedence over democratic interaction. One last theoretical observation before I get into some of the empirical side of things, and that is thinking about the way that the public realm intersects with violence. A lot of my work has focused on the geographies of violence and looking at how such geographical formations manifest in the context of Cambodia, and in relation to neoliberalism in particular. Something that the Cambodian government would conceptualize as "violence from below" could just as easily be called "resistance from below." So any sort of resistance activity can easily fit within the government's discourse of labeling it as "violence," and thus to be excluded from the public domain, whether legally or through shows of force by the government. They have the authority to define what is and is not "violence." Of course, the violence that they mete out against the population, they don't consider that as violence at all.

In Phnom Penh in the early 2000s, we saw a wave of forced evictions and dispossessions, particularly of what the government was calling squatter settlements. They legitimized these removals through their beautification agenda, or the Disneyfication of the public domain. The White Building in central Phnom Penh was a famous building that was, in many ways, at the epicenter of Cambodian resistance to what was, and what became, a national agenda to evict people from their homes and make way for capital investments. Those facing eviction are rarely reimbursed appropriately or properly compensated, and are routinely being denied any sort of claim to the land whatsoever. The White Building set the tone for how the government was to respond, but also laid a foundation for potential resistance to their "development" agenda. Police violence during evictions, and really also otherwise, is par for the course in Cambodia. Often, houses are lit on fire while people are still inside, and the people have to collect what they can before their homes are burned to the ground. Bulldozers are used, water cannons, all kinds of coercive tactics are put in place to recreate those spaces in such a way that the flow of capital can move forward, and those without significant political power are left by the wayside. Sadly, this is all too often what "development" looks like in Cambodia.

A very mundane example of the ordered view of the public realm that I mentioned before is that we'll see signs in public parks, basically instructing folks on the correct way to use those spaces versus the incorrect way to use those spaces. For example, playing soccer on the grass, not okay. Allowing your dog on the grass, or sitting on the grass, that's also not okay. You should be sitting on the bench as instructed, and that sort of thing. We might take these kinds of signs as a minor thing, but to push back on the script that the government has set for how public spaces are to be used is a form of everyday resistance, nonetheless. Cambodians do use the grass. They play soccer on it, they enjoy the existing public spaces in ways that are conducive to being together, and to enjoying each other's company, despite the instructions from the government.

Sopheap Chak: What I can say here, and reaffirm from what Simon has just presented, is the continuing crackdown on civic space. The civic space here is really broad, involving many actors, including journalists, the NGO (non-governmental organization) workers, young activists, and especially young environmental activists in the current moment. Many of these individuals have been arrested, and charged simply because they speak out on, for example, the issue of filling in the lake to make way for capital investment, or the waste that has been thrown into the river. The government crackdown on civic space here comes in many forms. One is through legal means, such as a number of legislative measures that the government has introduced, especially following the election in 2013. In that 2013 election, it was not about people supporting the opposition, per se. What people were really supporting is the idea of change because the ruling government had been in power for decades. Since that time, the government has introduced a number of restrictive legislations, like the Law on Associations and the NGO, that affects NGOs like us because the government believes

Figure 7.1
The ordered view of the public realm in Cambodia under the guise of environmental hygiene. Source: Simon Springer, 2004.

that this is a threat against their power. It is especially human rights organizations that have been empowering a larger population to understand that people have rights and people are entitled to exercise their freedom. With that law, the government has quickly chased out, for example, the National Democracy Institute. So, it is a form of intimidation.

Secondly, is the Trade Union Law. This law has targeted mostly at the unions, and garment factory workers. Before the election of 2018, the government used the taxation bill as a way to target and restrict the media. As a result, a number of independent publishers such as the long-running Cambodia Daily were forced to close their offices because of the liability for their tax bill. And that had been accumulating for over 10 years without anyone being informed. We lost credible media sources that played a very important role in Cambodians being kept informed. There have been also crackdowns on civic spaces of the public realm, via judicial harassment in which a number of young activists were recently arrested and charged. Last year in 2020, over 130 members of the opposition party were summoned to court at the same time. There are other forms of intimidation, such as violent crackdowns by police and military forces during protests. There was a latest case of the killing of a social analyst and political commentator, Kem Ley, who was killed while having coffee at a gas station. Former members of the opposition party, which was forcefully dissolved by the government, have been attacked physically and although they filed a formal complaint, there was no investigation or ultimately, justice, for them. There is also the use of direct threats or intimidation from senior government officials. We just had an urgent case regarding the Prime Minister's threat against a social analyst. He directly mentioned his name and said that he had to be careful about his

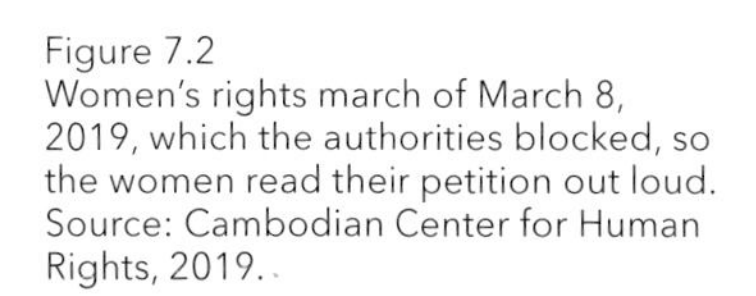

Figure 7.2
Women's rights march of March 8, 2019, which the authorities blocked, so the women read their petition out loud. Source: Cambodian Center for Human Rights, 2019.

analysis. Another form of intimidation is the surveillance of social media such as Facebook, Twitter, and Zoom meetings like we are doing right now.

This is the civic public space we are experiencing right now. It's really difficult in Cambodia because every move can be monitored, every move can be abused, or every move could result in jail time. This year, 2021, is the 30th anniversary of the Paris Peace Agreement, but the government tends to ignore the positive peace aspect. There is an obligation to make sure that Cambodia has complete peace by having both negative and positive peace. There is a need for us to understand and digest what peace really means. We know that there are risks ahead for us. The closing of civic public spaces that we have been experiencing so far is a result of the fact that the government believes that they can no longer manipulate or deploy a populist strategy anymore. So, where there are more people who rise up and when people become more aware, the government has to increase its repression to maintain its hold on power. Citizens are becoming more engaged and there is the hope, I believe, that this will continue. We also hope that new types of activists will enter the picture while active citizens continue to stay engaged. My hope lies in an active and activist citizenry.

Question: As media plays such a massive role, as in many regions, could you elaborate on how blocks to communication and awareness are overcome?

Sopheap Chak: I mentioned the change back in 2013 elections where the opposition gained certain

Figure 7.3
Peaceful protest in a public space in Phnom Penh in 2022.
Source: Cambodian Center for Human Rights, 2022.

momentum, and the rise of people demanding change resulting from the power of social media. So, it's not just about the traditional media who play the key role here, but social media has massively impacted the population. One is the access to information. In the past, because we had to rely a lot on traditional media, the risk of mind control was there, such as the plethora of propaganda by the government. Every time we turned on TV, we would see only what government officials did, such as inaugurating buildings like schools. But with Facebook, for example, we see many irregularities such as when people post about traffic police who take bribes from people. Or people would simply post a picture of violence against women that, in the past, the government would never take action. When certain photos are put up on Facebook, it really goes viral, and drives the government to take action. Still, we need professional media and that's why there has been an

effort from a number of actors, like civil-society organizations, to try to form independent media outlets to make sure that there is investigative journalism. Citizen journalists play an important role in the Cambodian context at the moment.

Question: I was wondering if you could talk a little bit more about the peace narrative that Sopheap mentioned in relation to control and order by the regime? Has the concept of "peace," in quotation marks, been instrumentalized to further oppress the Cambodian society? If so, are there efforts to reclaim "peace" as resistance?

Sopheap Chak: That's a good question, and it resonates with me deeply because we keep on trying to achieve this all the time, and when the media interviews me, I already have in my mind that it is not a complete peace. A complete peace requires not just the absence of war but fundamental freedoms and harmony that people can enjoy. In Cambodia it has become a slogan because every time the government accuses civil society actors like us or opposition who try to raise human rights issues, saying that our work negatively affects the prospect of achieving peace in the country. So, yes, "peace" has been instrumentalized.

I also mentioned about the Paris Peace Agreement. That is the foundation from which Cambodia can build a new country after the genocide. This year is the 30th anniversary of that Paris Peace Agreement. The government tried to argue that the agreement had been dead and was no longer relevant. But we, as civil society, try to remind the government that the Paris Peace Agreement is not only signed by Cambodia; it involves around 18 or 19 other countries. We keep calling for both the government and the member states who are signatories to the agreement to uphold their commitment to maintain peace in Cambodia. Because the document strongly defines peace as not just the absence of war. So the government has to commit to rebuilding the country based on human rights and democratic principles.

CO-DESIGN AS PARTICIPATION:

PROJECT 90 BY 2030, CAPE TOWN

LORNA FULLER

I'm Lorna; I work at Project 90 by 2030 as well, with a small team. There are eight of us in our team and we've been in Cape Town for a little while. Our theme in this presentation is co-design as participation and I've listened to lots of the talks yesterday and today in the symposium, and I feel like we have many similar challenges in the global south. We chose to focus on participation because that's a key pillar in our organization and I'm talking about it from a practitioner's point of view.

GABRIEL KLAASEN

My name is Gabriel Klaasen. I'm a 23-year-old activist from Cape Town, South Africa. I work at Project 90 by 2030 as the communications person. The reason that I found myself in communications at an NGO is because the focus of the organization is the injustices that we face in our communities on the ground here in Cape Town.

CHARLOTTE LEMANSKI

I'm at the University of Cambridge in the UK, and I'm a geographer. I've worked in and around South Africa, particularly Cape Town, for nearly 20 years, mostly working in low-income settlements, looking at issues around housing, infrastructure, and citizenship. Recently, I've been partnering with Jiska de Groot, who's a researcher at the University of Cape Town and with Project 90 by 2030, which is a NGO (non-governmental organization) based in Cape Town where both Lorna and Gabriel work.

Lorna Fuller: In terms of the context of Cape Town, we have quite a lot of disparity between the "haves" and the "have-nots." When we look at South Africa as a whole, we have 58.8 million people in the total population but half of the people in South Africa are living under the poverty line, and more than half of the youth under 24 years of age are unemployed. Our poverty rate is really high at 55 percent and linked to that are a lot of people who don't have access to, or cannot afford, electricity. That was our entry point since Project 90 by 2030 focuses on energy access and climate change. The other challenge that we face in South Africa is that we're only 30 years into democracy.

I see a lot of links to other speakers in the symposium over the last day-and-a-half. For example, we're still linked to colonialism, and we've got the added burden of apartheid as well. One thing that stands out for South Africa is that we have the highest Gini co-efficient, which means we're the most unequal country in the world, and that is actually quite astounding because when you see pictures of South Africa on the news, it often looks rosy. We've got a country with lots of beautiful aspects to it but hidden behind that is huge inequality, which is linked to our youth. Our youth unemployment is high, such that young people coming out of school often just don't get work. So, when we talk about public participation, we must bear in mind that this high inequality is perpetuated by a legacy of exclusion, which means that when we're talking about young people who are born into a poor family, chances are they will inherit that poverty line as well. I'm going to ask Charlotte to jump in here to talk about public participation in terms of theory and its global aspects.

Charlotte Lemanski: We've been thinking about co-design as a form of participation in this symposium. Most of us are aware of the word "participation" because we've heard it used either in our own lives or things that we've thought about in other countries. We already all come with our own assumptions about what we think we know participation is and how it's used to cover so many ways of consulting, communicating, working with, and partnering with people.

Over the last few decades, as neo-liberal decentralization and democratization agendas have come together it's created a global contemporary context where citizen engagement is explicitly promoted in governance processes around the world and participation of people is seen as central to a democratic governance process, at least in theory. In this kind of neo-liberal context, there's a real tension between the ways in which participatory governance is promoted for its instrumental value; that is, asking people their views, asking people to participate as a way of improving service delivery, resource distribution, and making the city work better for its citizens. But participation is also promoted for its intrinsic value, which is the idea that people's voices matter, people's views and perspectives and experiences are central to the city, and therefore they deserve to be heard, irrespective of whether this leads to greater efficiency or not.

Within this dichotomy, there is a tension as to the ways in which participation is used by different governments, different social movements, different NGOs, and different citizens. Participation can be a radical mechanism for citizens' voices to be heard, or a sneaky way for governments to be able to tick a box saying that we consulted people, or for governments and other organizations such as real estate developers to use the language of participation to in fact further marginalize the voices of those who are already marginalized or have different views or pursue forms of resistance . . . Let's now go back to Lorna to talk about participation in South Africa specifically.

Lorna Fuller: Active and engaged citizens are important, which is where our NGO, Project 90 by 2030, comes in and where the name is also our goal because we wanted a change of 90 percent by the year 2030 in our carbon emissions. And initially, we started off looking at our carbon emissions because they're linked to many social and environmental injustices.

As an organization we work with stakeholders and decision makers, and we try to identify policies and actions that support climate justice. We have a specific focus on developing environmental leadership in our youth and increasing people's ability to engage government through public participation to address climate change, energy poverty, and social injustices in their communities. We looked at energy and climate change because South Africa is the largest carbon emitter on our continent. In Africa we put out the most carbon, and that is because 80 percent of our electricity is generated from coal, which has its own environmental and social injustices that are linked to it.

At Project 90 by 2030, we have three spheres that we work in. We work in policy and research as a start because we want to share credible knowledge with our youth and community partners to help them move forward with their social movements. The other two skills are youth development and community partnerships. In policy and research, we talk about sharing the information as we collaborate with other NGOs to build a bigger footprint. There are so many people working around social injustice, but if we band together, we have a much stronger voice.

The four principles that we use in all of our areas are: collaboration, because we can't do it alone; leadership, because we're trying to encourage our youth and our community partners to be leaders in their areas; practical action, because you can't always wait for action to happen and sometimes you have to take action yourself; and communication in advocacy, to make sure everyone knows what you're doing. We not only look at participation through our policy work. For example, this is an image (see Fig 8.1) of one of our community leaders at a political debate where communities had the opportunity to ask the political candidates what their views were on energy access and climate change. This was organized by five different civil society organizations and we had seven political party leaders there, and they were targeted by our community leaders to answer some serious questions. We call it "community partnerships," because the activists that work with us know where they should be working and what their community needs since many of them have experienced activism for many years, especially with South Africa's history of political movements and youth taking to the streets. Community partnerships allow for peer-to-peer learning, to build campaigns, to take on public participation, and to write and engage with local government on energy and access to energy within their communities.

How does that link to the next principle, which is youth? We also have a youth mobilization aspect, and Gabriel Klaasen was actually one of our young members from our early climate change clubs that we had. He then became a mentor and recently he was an intern at Project 90 by 2030 and now as our communications officer, he knows how to spread the word within our communities and on social media. Gabriel is active in many climate change platforms, he's a representative of the African Climate Alliance, and he sits on the board of some other climate organizations as well.

The mobilization for next week (in September 2021) is a youth-led mobilisation. Everything's been organized by youth, including all the background work, and there's a team behind the scenes of older people, such as myself, just to support and to guide as need be. But the mobilization itself is a youth-led mobilization and that's what's so exciting. The whole theme is called "Uproot the DMRE" and the DMRE is our Department of Mineral Resources and Energy. The problem in South Africa is that the gatekeeper (i.e., the government) is holding on to coal and potentially looking at nuclear energy for the future, while all our renewable energy programs have been stalled–and that's where the youth are intervening right now. While I've been listening to the other talks at the symposium, I was trying to think what is different with Project 90 by 2030, and what we can add to these discussions is the power of youth. We believe that youth are real active citizens in addressing a lot of the issues and inequalities that

Figure 8.1
Community leader speaking at a political debate. Source: Project 90 by 2030, 2019.

we see. So, co-design is very interesting for us, because it's led us to think about how we do projects in the future to ensure that young people are part of the actual design process, and that participation is meaningful.

Question: I'm impressed with youth activism and their passion in climate change. I found it is like a trend, including in Cambodia, that young people are actively engaged in environmental and natural-resource protection. However, in some places this activism seems welcome, like with Greta Thunberg, who has gained a lot of worldwide support, young environmentalists elsewhere face threats and risk their lives. What should young communities do, as global citizens, to connect the space from one to another?

Lorna Fuller: Building solidarity is an inter-generational thing as I have found here in South Africa. For example, we're looking to activists from the anti-apartheid era to support the younger activists because many of the struggle issues are similar and they have a lot of knowledge of how things work. Another example is the African Climate Alliance, which is a group of young people who manage it and make the decisions, but in the background are some of the older generations who are there to support, to be mentors, to offer advice, and to do some practical stuff as well, such as to edit some of the op-eds that they write. I think young people are feeling exhausted and they feel like we are handing the burden of climate change specifically on to them to fix. It's like, "Here, we made a mess, you guys sort it out."

Question: I'm very interested in the question of time that came up yesterday in co-designing publics. Can you tell us a little bit about how you started your effort, your initiative, the organization, and how it has evolved over the years?

Lorna Fuller: For us to get meaningful participation in our communities or for our community activists to be able to participate, it takes a long time for them to build

Figure 8.2
YouLead Warriors: Young climate leaders mobilizing for their future.
Source: Project 90 by 2030, 2020.

their knowledge and to build their confidence. We've been working since 2007 in Cape Town and it's a lot of learning and re-learning. And we are learning by organizing but sometimes we make mistakes and sometimes we have small victories.

The current group of 12 activists have been working together since 2018 and we have great relationships with them. They

represent a whole array of communities in the Cape Flats area of Cape Town. The Cape Flats is very densely built, but it's one of the lowest-lying land areas in the city, and it faces all sorts of climatic conditions, such as extreme heat, extreme cold, winds, and in the future, sea level rises.

These activists come from those areas, and it's taken us a long time to build a partnership where we can honestly take that information and use it in our policymaking, and they feel safe enough to use our information to share in their communities and to build their movement. Currently, they're working on a free basic electricity campaign because people are allocated free basic electricity by our treasury department and in 2019, six billion South African rands was *not* actually handed out to people who deserved to have that money and that means that 5,600,000 people did not get their free basic electricity allocated money and that money was just reallocated in the municipalities.

These activists have now decided, as part of their 2021 campaign, to collect information in their communities to understand why people can't access their free basic electricity, and then to partner with us and other organizations to take on the policy of why it's so difficult for people to access their stuff. This is quite an interesting campaign and we're excited because it's their campaign and we are supporting them and so that's why we call it a community partnership. I'll see if Gabriel wants to add into that, being our communications person.

Gabriel Klaasen: I have been part of the spaces of many engagements and meetings since 2018 . . . Sometimes you come to a workshop with an objective and that workshop's objective gets thrown out the window because that week, it needs to be a de-briefing week due to changing circumstances. The reality is that when working with people and engaging in participation we've got to realize that the livelihoods are not separate from the activists' space and that you can't tell someone to leave their problems at the door and then come in. It doesn't work that way.

SUBVERSIVE AESTHETICS IN THE AMERICAS

MACARENA GÓMEZ-BARRIS

I am a writer and scholar with a focus on the decolonial environmental humanities, authoritarianism and extractivism, queer Latine epistemes, media environments, cultural theory, and artistic practice. I am the Timothy C. Forbes and Anne S. Harrison University Professor of Modern Culture and Media, and Chair of Modern Culture and Media at Brown University.

Question: Can you help us think through a little bit more how the incredible work that you're presenting and analyzing can help us rethink about what it means to co-design publics? You touched on it in bits and pieces, but can you help us think about that in terms of what does it mean to redefine what co-designing publics might mean in our day and age?

Macarena Gómez-Barris: I think one of the ways is by not assuming that we understand what poverty means, what marginalization means, or what oppression means, within our current frameworks. And to understand the pluriversality and immense resources in Black, Indigenous, and people of color communities. Also in relation to co-designing publics, it's so important to bring cultural memory to the foreground in order to really understand the coloniality of those histories. And to be able to fully engage creativity as multidimensional practices and important sites of disruption to the normative narration of these histories.

That's why I paused, for instance, on the importance of peace parks and the work they do for communities of witnesses. This is not just a past-oriented ossification of history as it is a permanent space of mourning, though such spaces also have other functions. But sites of memory and peace parks, especially when community oriented and designed, can become places for enlivening new connections among young people, and places for intergenerational education, as ways to imagine new artistic, aesthetic, and architectural representations of the histories of brutality. These are not healing places in a linear way, but places that recognize the impossibility of full healing and sites that account for, educate, and connect disparate communities and ways of reckoning with collective trauma and repair. We must consider the complexity of what we're contending with in the aftermath of colonialism, and the impossibility of fully contending with coloniality and its violence. Co-creation of architecture and indeed, the public realm, must commit to offering spaces for these deeper and multi-layered histories of racialized suffering, of the palimpsest of pain that lives in the soil.

Figure 9.1
Peace Park, Santiago de Chile. David Berkowitz, 2010, Wikimedia Commons.

10

CO-DESIGN AGAINST TRADITIONAL POWER STRUCTURES:

ASOMEVID, CALI

ALEXANDER LÓPEZ

I am a social community leader from Barrio Charco Azul. I have been a mental health promoter for the Secretariat of Health of Cali since 2001 and I am an assistant for the research project on rental housing in Colombia and the UK. As a social activist in Cali, I have coordinated the projects "Abriendo Caminos" and "Cure Violence," and I am currently involved in the research project "Social infrastructure and pandemic resilience." In recent years, I have worked on the vindication of rights with our organization ASOMEVID (Asociación Mejorando Vidas), through actions for the generation of inclusion, the right to housing, employment, and health.

MELANIE LOMBARD

I am a Senior Lecturer in the Department of Urban Studies and Planning at the University of Sheffield. My research agenda involves connecting the built environment to social processes through exploring the everyday activities that construct cities, often neglected by formal theories and practices of planning and urbanism. Under this broad agenda, two core themes of urban informality, and land and conflict, have emerged. I have explored these themes in cities in Latin America (Mexico and Colombia) and Europe (UK), and more recently have been interested in comparing these issues across diverse contexts, including in African cities. My current research explores the effects of the Colombian peace process on marginalized urban communities.

CARLOS TOBAR

I am a Professor at the Department of Communication and Language of the Faculty of Humanities and Social Sciences of the Pontificia Universidad Javeriana Cali, and coordinator of the Communication and Languages research group. In recent years, I have been dedicated to the study of social vulnerability in rural and urban communities in Valle del Cauca. I am a psychologist and communicator from the Pontificia Universidad Javeriana Cali, with a master's in philosophy from the Universidad del Valle and a PhD in social and cultural anthropology from the Autonomous University of Barcelona, Spain. I am currently a visiting Professor at the University of Sheffield, UK, and a researcher on the Contested Territories project of the European Union.

OVERVIEW

As part of our presentation, we first offer a partial contextualization of the city of Cali, Aguablanca District, and the impact of the National Strike in 2021. Later on, we describe our understanding of co-design in the public realm, especially as resistance against traditional power structures. We then present the case of ASOMEVID. Finally, we present our perspective on how to continue building processes of co-design.

CALI, AGUABLANCA, AND THE NATIONAL STRIKE IN 2021

Carlos Tobar: Cali is the administrative capital of the Valle del Cauca, an area of fertile land which is currently mainly used for the monoculture of sugar cane. Since 1990, there has seen significant growth due to migration caused by the armed conflict. In this context, Aguablanca District started to develop during the second half of the 20th century. Cali had a population of 1,822,871 inhabitants in 2018, around half of which are

Afro-Colombian. In fact, Cali is the Latin American city with the second-largest population of African descent, after Salvador de Bahía in Brazil. Aguablanca District is made up of four *comunas* or districts, housing approximately 455,790 people.

During the coronavirus pandemic, Resolution 385 was issued by Colombia's Ministry of Health and Social Protection, including a series of measures that introduced social distancing for the first time in Colombia's history, in order to prevent the spread of this dangerous disease. Social distancing affected access to food security.

There were already hunger issues in Aguablanca and social distancing exacerbated them. This situation was the starting point for the Colombian National Strike in 2021, whose trigger was the introduction of a tax reform by the national government that would worsen the economic situation of working-class neighborhoods (Indepaz, 2021). During the nearly three months of the strike in Cali, it became the setting for daily demonstrations in which local and regional groups took part, with a strong presence of young people, expressing their disagreement with Colombia's inequalities, lack of opportunities, and violence.

Alexander López: During the National Strike, we demonstrated in order to give visibility to our problems because we saw the strike as a tool to highlight all the issues we have in our communities. However, due to the circumstances of this strike, which was particularly acute in Cali, we also initiated a dialogue in order to limit damage to public space in our neighborhood by talking to young people to make them understand damage that was being caused to so many things we had achieved in many years of struggle. It was also important for us to show that there are in fact difficulties that need to become visible, to show that not all is well, and to recognize that there are internal conflicts, too.

CO-DESIGN AND THE PUBLIC REALM

Melanie Lombard: The work presented at the symposium addressed co-design as resistance against traditional power structures by considering it as a collaborative strategy for spatial transformation in circumstances negotiated by the community itself. We will now discuss the concepts of 'public realm,' 'power,' and 'co-design' to explore how these processes affected Aguablanca District within the context of the National Strike in Colombia.

The *public realm* is a concept that encompasses two very important dimensions: urban physical space and political space, in which decisions are made about communal living. To that effect, Escobar (2016) suggests that co-design should be understood as a process that recognizes the self-sufficiency and plurality of communities that come into play within its realm and contexts.

Latin America has a history of questioning and resistance in the public realm. During the 20th century, social movements occupied public space with demands for access to urban goods and services, frequently represented by marginalized and informal neighborhoods. Some examples of these are the *Movimiento Urbano Popular* in Mexico in the 1970s and 1980s, or the *Marcha del Ladrillo*, following the destruction of housing in Antioquia as part of the Colombian civil conflict. These examples played out not only in official urban spaces of the central city, but also in ordinary and informal spaces of peripheral neighborhoods. More recently, those spaces have been influenced by the surge in formal participation in urban government structures, since power in the public realm is also linked to issues of political economy regarding resource distribution in the production of the public space.

Both before and during the Covid-19 pandemic, we have seen the exacerbation of protests in Latin America. Some examples of this are the cases of social uprising in Chile, feminist protests in Mexico, and protests against the government in Cuba, as well as the Colombian National Strike in 2021. Such demonstrations involved occupying public space as a way to express claims about equitable access to goods and services, and important rights–including to education, to employment, and to live peaceful existence. Those were some of the goals of the Colombian National Strike from April to June 2021 (Indepaz, 2021).

Carlos Tobar: Young people, and in particular those who were not employed or in the education system, actively participated in this National Strike. These young people joined with groups of activists, workers, and other traditional sectors that had not previously participated in such processes. For example, university students demonstrated together with supporters of *Deportivo Cali* and *América de Cali*, local football teams with large numbers of supporters. Young people from marginalized neighborhoods in Aguablanca also played a significant role in this process. Over time, these young people developed alternative ways of expressing their social demands in the areas of culture and sport, thereby having an impact in the public realm.

NEIGHBORHOOD OF CHARCO AZUL AND ASOMEVID

Alexander López: Charco Azul is our home, and one of the neighborhoods of Aguablanca, in the east of the city of Cali. It has approximately 1,850 households and 8,000 inhabitants, and while some of them were displaced by violence, others came seeking better living conditions. Our struggle began since this displacement. We originally settled in the area in a space provided by a foreman looking after agricultural land on which the neighborhood was founded.

The struggle to own land was the first factor that motivated the fight against the state in the end of the second half of the 20th century. Access to land makes it possible for migrant families to organize, build new houses, and improve existing ones. The struggle was then for access to basic public services such as drinking water, sewerage, and electricity. Once those goals were achieved, we undertook initiatives where the lessons learned from previous struggles were used to inform processes in ASOMEVID's work.

ASOMEVID is a community-based organization that promotes public participation through practices based on consensus, focusing on these core areas: access to goods and services, social relations, and influencing the state and decision-making processes—which we explore further below. In 2003, when we started to have a more frequent interaction with the state, we were obliged to participate in a more formal manner and our organization became legally registered. We created a team with the leaders that took part in this process, focusing mainly on the Afro-Colombian population since 80 percent of our population is of African descent.

These different processes required development of specific social initiatives and community-focused methodologies based on diagnosis of needs, analysis of potential actions, and the assessment of prior experiences in order to improve on them. Our goal was to first see which issues affected the community the most, because there was a lot of confusion with regards to which needs to prioritize and disagreement about how we should fight for them. We thought that the struggle to improve our living conditions should be done in an organized way and therefore, we created what we called the triangle strategy. The first component of that triangle is access to goods and services, linked to the lack of meeting basic needs such as employment, education, housing, sport, etc. The second component is social and institutional relations, where we are in contact with leaders, organizations, public and private entities, etc. The last component is access to

Figure 10.1
Parque El Separador.
Source: ASOMEVID's Photographic archive, 2021.

power and decision-making spaces, which is about being able to take part in such spaces of power. This strategy has been effective for the organization because it has allowed inclusion of community demands in local government departments where budgets are implemented to improve marginalized neighborhoods.

The focus on access to decision-making spaces allowed us to progress in our struggle. For instance, one of our main initiatives was called *Yo Soy El Presidente* (I Am the President). This initiative allowed the community to be empowered and take part in contexts where decisions are made, through the nomination of diverse community members as members of the local Junta de Accion Comunal, which is the formal neighborhood committee. This allowed people to say 'no' to having the same leader year after year, and 'yes' to empowerment, to appropriating spaces, to active participation, and to coming together in order to maintain the public realm. We no longer had a traditional committee

Figure 10.2
Parque El Quemado before and after intervention.
Source: ASOMEVID's Photographic archive, 2021.

where there is only one president who receives all the demands, instead we are an empowered community where everyone can say: 'I'm the president.'

This strategy allowed us to access the Local District Committee, the entity that interfaces with neighborhood committees with the departments of the Cali city council. The neighborhood committee also became a tool to exercise power in two directions. On the one hand, we exercised the power of organizing through strategies such as *Yo Soy El Presidente* for residents to access decision-making spaces. On the other hand, we have been able to make claims on municipal institutions and create a sense of community appropriation of municipal decision-making spaces. Those two ways of working have allowed us to carry out our actions in order to improve our neighborhood.

For example, our participation in neighbourhood planning committees has had an impact on local budgets. Parque El Separador is an example of this where, thanks to our efforts, we have managed to achieve these changes. Parque El Separador

is a park in the center of the neighborhood. It was transformed in 2017 through the efforts of ASOMEVID, supported by the community, to cover over a drainage channel that flowed through the neighborhood. The culverting of the drainage channel and the construction of the park led to the creation of this important public space with a children's play area and green space that residents use for leisure and social purposes.

Another recent example of transformation of urban space is that of the Parque El Quemado, through a successful process of dialogue with public bodies. In this case, we worked with the Department of Infrastructure, the Planning Department, and with decision-making bodies such as the Planning Committee. Parque El Quemado was an abandoned housing plot that had been the site of murders and rapes; a negative space that we then transformed into a positive space. This transformation process was done with young people who had been involved in some of the negative situations, since there is no point in transforming space without the element of appropriation.

CO-DESIGN FROM ASOMEVID'S POINT OF VIEW: IDEAS TO CONTINUE BUILDING

Alexander López: We see co-design from two points of view in the social practices that occur in Aguablanca. The first one is vertical power, which involves convening cross-sectoral partnerships and being present in the organizations of the state in order to ensure that external interventions have a positive impact on our community. The second is horizontal power within the neighborhood of giving visibility to vulnerable groups and issues associated with the structural injustices of the Colombian armed conflict. Through these social struggles, we have sought to empower our community and develop potential actions in line with our identity as an organization, because it doesn't make sense to fight for institutions to do or build something (e.g., a park) if no sense of ownership is created. There is also an important element that differentiates ASOMEVID from other organizations: trust, which involves knowing that decisions made by a member of the organization won't negatively affect the rest of us. This is a guiding principle in the organization; that is, finding ways to act without negatively affecting others.

We would especially like to highlight ASOMEVID's ability to generate consensus and build networks to support collaborative work. The underlying idea here is, "We can negotiate with everyone, including seeking negotiations that might initially appear impossible." These processes of consensus-building can be understood as temporary and limited; that is, there is no permanent consensus, only those that exist in response to particular opportunities.

Carlos Tobar: Colombia's history tells us that no consensus can last forever, instead it needs to be recreated continually, and more so when the relationship with the state is fraught and generates multiple local and territorial political identities. This understanding fits into a Latin American tradition in which the goal of social protest is to provide visibility to needs of vulnerable populations through situations of dispute with the state. These situations aim to provide an understanding of social needs through which the rule of law will be secured.

ASOMEVID's experiences highlight its understanding that power is a balance between forces in conflict and where the idea of building consensus reveals innovative social practices in which political and physical spaces intersect. While the former responds to highlighting social needs and the agency of the organization, the latter corresponds to the achievements of dialogue with local government agents, through which resources are obtained for urban transformation.

Melanie Lombard: More work is needed on how both dimensions of the public realm–political space and physical space–interact, and how this is the basis for potential initiatives by community agents. This will require further exploration of the tensions between dominant state power and popular initiatives that seek to question it, and to extend options for representation of community needs. We suggest that political space can offer an area of temporary and limited consensus within a wider context characterized by risks and conflicts. This can be seen in the achievements of cross-sectoral partnerships that enabled the creation of public space, such as those undertaken by ASOMEVID, as well as in processes of protest, which play out in and may threaten the very public space that is co-created by communities. Understanding co-design against traditional power structures therefore requires paying attention to power, understood as a balance between forces.

Question: I would like to ask how this idea of conflict versus consensus works in practice. Does getting involved in conflict situations reduce the state's willingness to cooperate with your group?

Alexander López: What we have seen is that many times the state proposes solutions to problems that they assume exist in the neighborhood, but don't match reality. For example, the Department for Sport proposed the implementation of a swimming program. We replied that we couldn't implement a swimming program, but they insisted and sent us a swimming instructor who later realized that we didn't have a swimming pool. When the secretary arrived in Charco Azul and saw what was available in the area, it completely changed his perception of what our needs are. So, one of the ways to arrive at consensus is by showing and getting to know the real-life situations that we experience in the community.

Carlos Tobar: The realization of these consensus practices takes place in the public realm. Above all, in order to build a park or to carry out an action, you need to generate cross-sectoral partnerships that involve engagement with the state since they hold the budget, but also with the groups who inhabit these spaces. Therefore, these cross-sectoral partnerships start to influence the public realm. On the other hand, in the case of conflict, we see different expressions of social protest. I think the best example of how social protest becomes a space to give visibility to social conflicts is the National Strike, where people from different backgrounds demonstrated and expressed their discontent in a way they had never done before.

Melanie Lombard: To supplement this, I think that on the one hand, there is perhaps a history of a dual-organizational strategy in Latin America, where community-based organizations take part in protests on the one hand and, on the other, there are official channels to ask for goods and services. So, both spaces can coexist. On the other hand, I would also say, as Carlos pointed out, that Colombia is currently in a very specific historic moment. In fact, even though the peace process and peace accord may have stagnated with President Iván Duque's government, you could say that it's also a moment of openness for civil society. I think that the National Strike is also an example of this.

REFERENCES

Arana-Castañeda, C. A. (2020). Ausencia y presencia estatal como forma de reproducción de la violencia urbana en el Distrito de Aguablanca (Cali, Colombia).
Revista CS, (32), 77–102.
www.doi.org/10.18046/recs.i32.3910

Dane (2019). Results from the National Census of Population and Housing 2018, Cali, Valle del Cauca.
www.dane.gov.co/files/censo2018/informacion-tecnica/presentaciones-territorio/190711-CNPV-presentacion-valle.pdf

Escobar, A. (2016). La realización de lo comunal. Tinta Limón.
www.tintalimon.com.ar/public/t9924e4gnhfdarefj529d4ikr8r8/pdf_978-987-3687-27-3.pdf

Indepaz. (2021). Violence statistics within the framework of the national strike in 2021.
www.indepaz.org.co/wp-content/uploads/2021/06/3.-INFORME-VIOLENCIAS-EN-EL-MARCO-DEL-PARO-NACIONAL-2021.pdf

Ministry of Health and Social Protection of Colombia. (2020). Resolution 385 of the 12th March 2020.
www.minsalud.gov.co/Normatividad_Nuevo/Resoluci%C3%B3n%20No.%200385%20de%202020.pdf

DO IT RESPONSIBLY OR DON'T DO IT AT ALL

PANTHEA LEE

I am a practitioner, and I have deep respect and admiration for all the work that academics do. I offer some of my reflections as someone who's just been doing this type of work for the last 15 years as a journalist, as an ethnographer, as a facilitator, as a strategist. A lot of my work has been international, working between activists, community groups, international agencies, governments to try and help them co-design initiatives together. I currently do this work to champion visions of a more just, caring, and equitable world as the Co-Founder and Executive Director of Reboot.

Panthea Lee: As activists, oftentimes when we show up at a negotiating table, we are very quick to jump to our talking points in ways that are antagonistic and alienate those that we need on our side. This puts people in power on the defensive from the get-go, making it difficult for them to later concede–that is, for them to sign onto our demands. So, how do we name the tensions in more productive ways, how do we invite engagement? We must think about this in terms of how we show up.

Ethnographic studies show that in a lot of civic engagement processes, participants who have not traditionally had power often leave actually feeling more disengaged and less willing to participate in future processes. This is because there's a certain way of speaking and there's a certain way of presenting that they soon realize they don't know; and that is disempowering. Workshop participation nowadays is a skill, such as how to write a post-it and how to talk in soundbites. We need to break out of these debilitating norms and instead work more on creative ways to develop a shared point of view, or define common struggles from different point of views, in ways that center those with lived experience. How do we support and really enable folks to share

Panthea Lee 李佩珊 @PantheaLee · Aug 4, 2020
I have 5 invites in my inbox to "co-create the future".

I've architected, negotiated, led a lot of **co-creation** work. True **co-creation**. With stakeholders from diverse backgrounds (regionally, economically, politically, culturally) + some that hate each other.

What I've learned:

37 1,075 2,157

Panthea Lee 李佩珊 @PantheaLee · Aug 4, 2020
Replying to @PantheaLee
Co-creation is not throwing a bunch of people into a space / process / initiative and expecting magic to happen.

That's wishful thinking—and usually comes from a place of privileged myopia.

3 55 426

Panthea Lee 李佩珊 @PantheaLee · Aug 4, 2020
Co-creation is not gathering ideas from a bunch of people, then figuring out what you do with them later.

That's a consultation. One that is at best poorly planned, and at worst highly insulting.

2 36 345

Panthea Lee 李佩珊 @PantheaLee · Aug 4, 2020
Co-creation is not gathering inputs, realizing (inevitably) that most people don't see eye-to-eye, so presenting a diluted synthesis or lowest common denominator "solution" as the answer.

That's a waste of everyone's time—and how we abet mediocrity + sustain a toxic status quo.

2 30 318

Panthea Lee 李佩珊 @PantheaLee · Aug 4, 2020
So dear god please don't call it co-creation unless you're willing to invest—to really, truly invest—in a process that:

2 27 242

Panthea Lee 李佩珊 @PantheaLee · Aug 4, 2020
1. Calls out + tackles power imbalances—and doesn't ask those with less power to perform their trauma for institutional attention.

Those w/ privilege must first do the damn work to figure out what's broken. Those w/ lived experience then get to say what should be done about it.

3 56 489

Panthea Lee 李佩珊 @PantheaLee · Aug 4, 2020
2. Reckons with historical justices—and their present-day impacts. Because honestly, fuck "beginner's mindset".

(Aside: I was raised Buddhist + am deeply insulted by the corporate desig appropriation of this concept + its use to justify harmful, neocolonial, bullshit practices)

5 26 367

Panthea Lee 李佩珊 @PantheaLee · Aug 4, 2020
3. Leans into tensions, confronts controversy, and helps everyone (even avowed enemies) develop a shared point of view. THIS IS THE WORK!!!

It's damn tough. But we're grappling with power, upheaval, and renewal. it's not hard and uncomfortable, it's probably not worth doing.

4 39 380

Panthea Lee 李佩珊 @PantheaLee · Aug 4, 2020
4. Invests real resources in standing up what comes out of the process, whether those funding / sanctioning like it or not.

Power likes to hold on to power. Real structural solutions will challenge that. So do as much as you can to negotiate resources / signoffs in advance.

2 24 306

Panthea Lee 李佩珊 @PantheaLee · Aug 4, 2020
There's so much interest now in co-creation. That's a good thing.

Because systems that enable and sustain injustice, inequality, oppressio were intentionally designed. Futures that honour and protect justice, equity, liberation can also be designed.

But it requires all of us.

1 44 333

Panthea Lee 李佩珊 @PantheaLee · Aug 4, 2020
None of us on our own have the answers. Systems change requires communities, artists, activists, civil society, academics, governments, companies to reimagine together.

But we can't if all we get are co-opted processes + no real resources behi the emergent visions.

Do better.

17 70 458

Figure 11.1 Twitter Thread. Source: Panthea Lee, 2020.

their experiences and their truths in ways that will be heard?

Let's consider what co-design *is not*. Co-design is not throwing a bunch of people into a space together and expecting magic to happen. Co-design is not about gathering a bunch of inputs from different people and then figuring out what we do with them afterwards. Co-design is not processes where we gather inputs, realize inevitably that folks do not see eye to eye and that there's a lot of differences of opinion, and then try to incorporate everything into a Christmas-tree-type outcome. This yields a bad, lowest-common-denominator solution that doesn't really have a point of view, because we're trying to accommodate everyone's needs.

Here are some humble offerings about what co-design *does require*. We need to think about designing structures that do not put all that emotional labor and work on folks that do not have power. We as conveners and those with resources and power must first do the work to get a basic understanding of what's wrong. And then to bring in those with lived experiences to say what should be done. More and more, I'm thinking about how we reckon with historical injustices and their present-day impacts in these processes.

This can mean bringing in research and data and really asking the hard questions of why there is such a great power differential between the groups present in the first place, and what do we do about it? I also think about: Are the groups I'm working with willing to lean into the tensions and to develop a shared point of view that they may challenge their dominance? This is really hard work. If it's not hard and uncomfortable, it's not worth doing. So how do we actually get into processes where we can confront the lineages we have inherited? Finally, this to me is the most important: How do we invest real resources in standing up for what is coming out of the process? And so how do I do that due diligence for the communities that I am going to be asking to engage?

What should our future look like? I want our artists with their power of radical imagination, with their ability to see beyond our current depressing present and to articulate futures that are beautiful and joyous and delicious, to help set that north star for us. I want our activists with their moral clarity and courage setting the agendas. And we need community groups with their incredible creativity and generosity and agility and flexibility and love, showing us different mechanisms and models and paths to realizing this future. And academics and researchers bringing their intellectual rigor and their deep knowledge to help us map these paths to getting there. And then finally we bring companies and governments with their scale and resources and durability to organize markets and to set policies to help us move forward.

Question: In your field and given your identity, how do you and those around you try and succeed in pushing through in a space where we're not a part of the original design?

Panthea Lee: The work of Generative Somatics, a wonderful organization based out of the west coast of the United States, has been really helpful for my work in this area. They do a lot of work in helping folks learn how to embody change and stand in our power. In discovering their work and the work of Staci K. Haines, one of the founders who wrote this brilliant book called *The Politics of Trauma*, I thought a lot about how most of our notions of empowerment are actually quite superficial. I realized as a facilitator and as a mediator, this is the work that I need to do to be able to show up well for myself and for all the groups that I'm trying to facilitate and to push back against problems in ways that are really meaningful in the moment.

Question: In the case of journalists and the media, which you know a lot about, how can narratives be pushed to seek social change, and how could new public agendas be formed?

Panthea Lee: I think those of us on the left are not particularly coordinated in terms of our messaging strategy. We're a bit of "let a thousand flowers bloom," and "pluralism is great," and

Figure 11.2 Training program that "Generative Somatics" was part of in Latin America. Source: IDWF, 2019, Flickr.

"look at all the beautiful colors of people and multiculturalism and multifaith." I don't necessarily think that this is a good strategy to counter the fear that some white people have that their power is going away, a strategy seeded by elites and white supremacists that seek authoritarian power. So what's the work that white people have to do in telling stories to each other? I think narrative changes are where the fight needs to be right now. Artists have an incredible amount to offer here, but they're often not taken seriously in these spaces; we typically consider their value more in social protest art than in actually setting new visions and worlds. But as Toni Cade Bambara says, "The role of the artist is to make revolution irresistible." We need to tap into this.

Question: I believe we also need to bring those conversations to funding decisions, which are often way before the design process. So, I want to ask you to comment on that.

Panthea Lee: I think the fact that–and this is more United States-specific–concepts like abolition and reparations are part of mainstream policy debates, this is really exciting. And this is a result of protests and of mass mobilization. I think for those of us working in this space, the question is how we can be useful allies because activists are very good at saying, "The framing of the problem is wrong and the money is not enough," but what activism often struggles with is, "What are the specifics of what we *do* want." We're good at saying what we don't want, but we're not good at saying okay then, "What comes next?" Funders and others with access to elite power structures can help map political and technical strategies, with more insider knowledge than grassroots groups. This is essential to change, as is resourcing the movements that are actually driving the ground game.

CO-DESIGNING PUBLICS INTERNATIONAL SYMPOSIUM:

CLOSING THOUGHTS

CHARLOTTE LEMANSKI

In this concluding talk, I will attempt to draw the two days (i.e. September 16-17, 2021) of this symposium together. It's been a long two days. A brilliant two days. A fantastic, rich, interesting two days. What I want to do in this closing section is firstly to do a very short summary and reflection on each of the core talks that we had from the Co-Designing Publics research network partners because due to time zones in different parts of the world that people attended online, not everyone could attend every talk. Secondly, I also want us to think across those talks about what is co-design, what does it mean in practice, as well as all the contestations, different actors, and different roles that are involved; and finally, to ask some quite difficult questions. I'll start by providing a summary of each of the six talks that we had on co-design: as engagement with the city, as a long-term process, as contestation of power, as resistance, as participation, and against traditional structures of power.

We started with thinking about co-design as engaging with the city. We had a very rich empirical story from the Rujak Center for Urban Studies, who work with the urban poor in Jakarta, especially dealing with issues of poverty and climate change. Their amazing example of community planning and rapid assessment was so fascinating and insightful in terms of designing a Community Action Plan that was co-designed with the community with no government involvement. After presenting the plan to the government, the government appropriated it and appeared to claim it as their own, with the governor attending the launch and the provincial government branding it as their event.

This was a self-led process that often in many cases around the world we see as a kind of contestation and conflict with the state, with citizens making their own plans, developing their own ideas, and the state often opposing that. But in this example, the city not only legitimized what communities had done themselves, but in one sense effectively claimed what was actually a community-based program. What, then, does it mean when co-design is engagement with the city? In the Jakarta example, they talked about the way that co-designing an engagement requires learning, but it also requires unlearning. Habits that we have and assumptions that we make must be challenged, and that there needs to be a leveling of hierarchies to accept that everyone is learning together in order to truly engage with the city. Reflecting on the issues related to climate change in Jakarta, this presentation raised the idea that co-design is not just between people, such as communities or the state, but that there are also non-human actors and participants and stakeholders in co-design–such as the very materiality of the city.

In terms of co-design as a long-term process, we saw the example of Hasiru Dala (i.e., Green Force in the regional Kannada language) in Bengaluru, who work with waste pickers to challenge the stigmas of waste pickers as dirty, uneducated, and unprofessional. It was exciting to hear their innovative use of language–defining these workers as semi-skilled entrepreneurs providing a key service rather than as waste pickers. The way that they talked about and practiced co-design cut across three different spheres: the political, the spatial, and the temporal; and it was important to them that all three aspects be present when thinking about co-design.

What was really interesting about the way they told a story about co-design was that it wasn't just about transplanting waste entrepreneurs into government negotiations, it was actually about education; educating the non-waste pickers; educating government officials; and more broadly, educating middle-class citizens about the role that waste entrepreneurs do play in maintaining the city and can play in other government processes. It was also interesting to think about the process of convincing citizens that the reason this inclusion needed to happen was because of the sustainability benefits. Using the language of the middle class and of state officials, which is the language of "environmental sustainability," was one way to legitimize the role of waste entrepreneurs in discussions around the future of the city in which they are already functioning. Hasiru Dala also gave some interesting examples about the spatiality of co-design in the city, such as how creating a physical dry-waste collection center led to female empowerment and how discarded waste materials became a material mechanism to co-design spaces of the city. Most of all, we started to think about temporality and spoke about the fact that in order to develop co-design, it takes long-term relationships and trust building through collective processes.

Next, we started to think about co-design as contestation of power, with examples from União dos Movimentos de Moradia (i.e., Union of Housing Movements in Portuguese) in São Paulo about how working with grassroots organizations can play a role in contesting power structures. These examples challenged systemic inequalities through pressuring public powers from the outside to engage in forms of institutional participation that the state had established. In addition, communities developed their own alternatives collectively and as part of the co-design process, pressured the government to legitimize such community-led solutions. Like with Hasiru Dala, it was vital to make sure that wider urban society understands why they have a primary stake in co-design, even if they benefit indirectly rather than directly through the actions of the União. They talked about training and capacity building, not just of low-income communities but also of government officials, middle-class residents, academic scholars, and community activists. In fact, often, it is low-income communities that need to learn the least since they already know what it's like to be marginalized, what it's like to be excluded, and they tend to know what they want and that they don't seem to be able to get it through standard channels that seemed to work for other groups of people.

The discussion on co-designing as resistance from the Cambodian Center for Human Rights took us to Cambodia, where the Cambodian government has a very strong emphasis on ordered stability as the normative framework for how society should function within a very neoliberal economic format. And arguably the public realm as a space for resistance is incredibly problematic within that context. Resistance is seen as unwelcome, and "uncivic" if you like, and therefore, the idea of the public realm as a space for resistance is problematic for the Cambodian state. In other words, what the government is saying, in effect, is that "we've created peace in this country, and your resistance is challenging the peace that is here, you are disrupting the ordered stability that your ancestors fought for." The irony is the state using that as a narrative in the context of incredibly high state forms of violence, as if the state is somehow above this narrative of peace.

We have this conflicting rationality in the sense that citizens understand themselves to be expressing their human rights, which the state considers as resistance and therefore there's been a significant state crackdown on civic and digital spaces of resistance. In this presentation, there was also a lot of reflection on hope. Is resistance a way of thinking about hope? I wanted to challenge us to think a little bit about more everyday forms of resistance and the ways in which resistance can often be undertaken by people in their everyday lives in very small and incidental ways.

We then came to co-design as participation, shifting to Cape Town in contemporary post-apartheid South Africa, where extreme inequality remains dominant. South Africa is quite radical in that participation is a constitutional right and there aren't many countries around the world where the right of citizens to participate in decision making is embedded in the constitution. Yet, in practice, often that participation does not materialize for low-income and marginalized groups because it is mediated through established non-governmental groups (NGOs), through elite groups, and through middle-class groups.

Project 90 by 2030 is a relatively small NGO in Cape Town, and yet has had a significant impact by working with activists and with youth to try and bring about community activism and capacity building, and to infiltrate government decision making. It was insightful to hear about challenges in how ongoing inequalities make it extremely difficult for poor communities to be able to access participation, whether that's due to very tangible factors such as inability to access transport to get to a meeting or to access the internet, but also perhaps less tangible in terms of the deep-rooted trauma that many communities and many people face in South Africa, and the inability of those people to overcome that in order to negotiate and consult with a government that's itself deemed to be the perpetrator of significant trauma, exclusion, violence, and marginalization. Participation has almost become a word that people are ashamed to use in South Africa because of the negative connotations that it has in this context. Whereas co-design, co-production, and collaboration are perhaps now seen as more appropriate, because they suggest a more equal, more level playing field. Could co-design be a more appropriate way to engage communities in decision making about their lives, and about the city?

Finally, we shifted to ASOMEVID (i.e. Asociación Mejorando Vidas, or Association for Improving Lives in Spanish) in Cali, Colombia, thinking about co-design as a way of rallying against traditional structures of power. The Cali example was absolutely fascinating because of the significant history of armed conflict and youth mobilization in public spaces that the city has seen. Alex introduced us to the community group ASOMEVID, which is a great example of a long-term process, and the incremental way in which what is a very small community group has gone from winning the right to occupy space to becoming registered with the state, developing a logo and a set of three goals: to access goods and services, to access social institutions, and to access decision-making processes, especially at the state. We were all fascinated at the end of the presentation by the idea of co-design against traditional structures of power by bringing together consensus and conflict, not seeing them as contradictory or opposing but thinking about how to balance them.

In this summary, I wanted to remind us of all the talks, case studies, and different cross-cutting questions and to think about what that they might mean for us next, as individuals, with the partners that we work with, but also as a research and practice network. This has been a network that we've developed over the last few months, and we have had a series of interactive and collaborative workshops, with this international symposium as a kind of final public workshop. We've worked across Australia, Brazil, Cambodia, Colombia, India, Indonesia, South Africa, the UK, and the USA. I decided to mention the countries, because what I want to demonstrate here is that this is a network that has traversed significant institutional differences, cultural experiences, multiple time zones, and languages. Despite all those significant differences, we've found resonance in thinking about co-design, and thinking about the public realm.

I'm going to go through the questions that I've put up on the slide as a springboard for us to then have a discussion.

- Is the messy, conflictual, and antagonistic nature of co-design a hindrance or asset?
- Is co-design always a long-term process or can short-term interventions be effective?
- Is community-initiated co-design more 'democratic' than state-initiated co-design?

- Who is in co-design? The right humans or the right titles and roles?
- How can those in places of privilege help mitigate the dangers of co-design (e.g., state surveillance, violence, oppression) and lack of financial remuneration?
- What are we co-designing? (e.g., urban spaces, urban governance, resource distribution, communities, scholarship, activism?)
- Is co-design about the outcomes or the process?
- What are the implications of co-design for scholarship, teaching, activism, and practice?
- What is the hope of co-design?

The first is that it's very clear that co-design is not simple. You don't walk into a room, tick a box, and say, aha, co-design. It's messy, conflictual, antagonistic, people disagree with each other, people have different ways of doing things.

My second question is encouraging us to think again about this idea of temporality. There's been a broad consensus amongst the presentations and amongst the experiences shared that co-design is a long-term process. I wondered if we could push that a bit more and think about whether long term is always preferable, whether there are sometimes short-term benefits. We could think about whether long-term processes have implications for youth involvement and could be exclusionary, whether they could lead to inertia as people might give up over time, whereas kind of shorter campaigns can get people more committed.

The third question is thinking about co-design as something that is state-initiated versus community-initiated. We may need to challenge that assumption and to argue that there are different types of co-design, and not that some are necessarily superior or inferior, and that embracing a broader starting point for co-design might open up more possibilities and more conversations.

The fourth question is something that was raised for me by Panthea Lee's talk, which is, "Who is in co-design?" She had this great phrase, which was "Do we want the right humans or the right titles and roles?" Thinking about who are the people that we're targeting in co-design, are we talking about academics and practitioners, government and academics, government and practitioners?

The fifth question is something that came up in many presentations but often as an aside rather than as a main argument, which was that there are real, including political, risks to being involved in co-design. We can therefore think about what role those of us in places of privilege, and I certainly put myself in the bracket as someone at the University of Cambridge, can play in trying to help mitigate those risks and the lack of financial remuneration that often comes with participating in processes of co-design.

The sixth question is thinking about, "What are we co-designing?" In terms of the project, we took our starting point as the public realm. Some of it could be space, some of it is about politics, about urban governance, and some of it could be about resource distribution. Are we co-designing communities? Can we co-design scholarship? Are we co-designing activism? [Editor's note: As the title of this book suggests, co-designing "publics" is the focus of this particular network, which was defined in the introductory talk and opening essay, but much more implicitly discussed in the other talks and essays.]

Question seven is for us to think about, "What's more important in co-design? Is it the outcome where we're talking about trying to transform the city, or transform the academy? Or is the process of co-design in and of itself, equally as important or maybe more important?" The process and discussion of co-designing was itself valid and important because it did bring about change in all of us, in terms of the ways that we practice, and the ways in which we understood the issues that we have been talking about.

Question eight is a wrapping-up type of question: "What are the implications of co-design for scholarship, teaching, activism, and practice?" I know at the start Aseem talked about radical democracy, which made me think about a concept that Edgar Pieterse, who's the head of the African Center for Cities, proposed, which is radical incrementalism. Which of course, sounds like an oxymoron: if something is radical, how on earth can it be incremental? What he is talking about with that phrase is that change in the city and in governance processes does not happen fast. It happens gradually, but it does need to be radical. The idea of radical incrementalism is bringing temporality into co-design and saying that while we do need radical change, maybe we need to accept that it doesn't always happen quickly. It takes time, but that can still be radical.

Comment: How do we think democracy and citizenship relate to the themes of the public realm and co-design? I think this is especially relevant in context of informality, where perhaps we can't take these concepts or these ideas for granted in any way.

Comment: I genuinely appreciate the lesson that I'm taking into my own personal upliftment and upskilling, but also into the way that we in the Project 90 by 2030 group in Cape Town group work going forward.

Comment: I think something that's also been implicit in all our discussions has actually been the question of power, which is part of this process, in terms of shifting the center where power sits. It's something that I'm keen to build out and take forward, and see how as academics, we can actually put some of this material out there that can be open access that can be used in ways that can help groups kind of build on some of the work that we've been doing as toolkits. [Editor's note: A huge part of making our work accessible has been the website and the free and open-to-the-public international symposium, and this edited book, which––while not totally free–will be affordable, accessible, and engaging for a broad audience.]

Comment: In co-designing with youth to tackle something like the climate catastrophe, we have general discussions about offering them opportunities to be heard and to learn a little bit more. I'm hoping that we can move faster as we learn all the sorts of social issues that the youth want to tackle, and that we can support them with the time aspect of it. In terms of time, some projects you can do quickly and some are going to take a longer time.

Comment: I was just going to build on the previous statement. It struck me that part of the reason that you can sometimes do things in a short timeframe is because you've already got the long-term engagement. For example, building relationships is always long-term, I don't think anybody can dispute that. But that can sometimes be a foundation on which to bring about short-term activities.

13

EPILOGUE

ASEEM INAM

I want to wrap up our gathering at this international symposium with a few comments. As Evaniza Rodrigues said quite powerfully earlier, "We are changing the world and changing the way that the world is changing." This brings us to the last question in Charlotte Lemanski's thought-provoking slide: "What is the hope of co-design? Where is the hope of co-design?" I think hope is not just in the future; it's very much in the present. All the amazing work that we saw presented in the workshops earlier and then at this symposium is emblematic of hope, which is happening now. The remarkable work that all of you are doing in these cities (i.e., Bengaluru, Cali, Cape Town, Jakarta, Phnom Penh, São Paulo) is inspiring for all of us. That is one of the principal goals of this research network–to learn from each other.

We bring about change in small ways and large ways, sometimes collectively, sometimes individually. The hope is right here in front of us now, right in front of our noses, and what we have to do is to constantly look for it and build on it, as we move forward. Finally, while there was quite a bit of discussion about "co-design," we should not forget an equally powerful concept and practice, which is that of "publics," as described in the opening presentation. Publics are heterogeneous and fluid, and if we understand this reality, we can organize and mobilize our communities around specific issues and over time in a heterogenous and fluid manner. We all belong to and co-create multiple communities, and we can similarly co-design multiple and potent publics in places that we care about.

ORO Editions
Publishers of Architecture, Art, and Design
Gordon Goff: Publisher

www.oroeditions.com
info@oroeditions.com

Published by ORO Editions

Author: Aseem Inam
Book Design: Ahankara Art
Managing Editor: Jake Anderson

10 9 8 7 6 5 4 3 2 1 First Edition

ISBN: 978-1-957183-57-2

Color Separations and Printing: ORO Group Ltd.
Printed in China.

ORO Editions makes a continuous effort to minimize the overall carbon footprint of its publications. As part of this goal, ORO Editions, in association with Global ReLeaf, arranges to plant trees to replace those used in the manufacturing of the paper produced for its books. Global ReLeaf is an international campaign run by American Forests, one of the world's oldest nonprofit conservation organizations. Global ReLeaf is American Forests' education and action program that helps individuals, organizations, agencies, and corporations improve the local and global environment by planting and caring for trees.